Praise for *The Atheist's Way*

"Millions of people lead happy, moral, loving, meaningful lives without believing in a god, and Eric Maisel explains in exquisite rational and compassionate detail how we do it. Instead of a purpose-driven life, atheists have life-driven purpose: we don't find meaning — we make meaning. After reading Maisel's thoughtful, informed arguments, backed up with real-life success stories, you will be utterly convinced of the 'pointlessness of pointlessness.'"

— Dan Barker, author of *Godless: How an Evangelical Preacher Became One of America's Leading Atheists* and co-president of the Freedom from Religion Foundation

"Books advocating atheism can sometimes be hard, dogmatic, or angry. Not this one. Maisel's fresh and unique contribution is inviting, engaging, and downright soulful. Rather than hammering away at the irrationality of belief, debunking the Bible, or regurgitating standard arguments against theism, *The Atheist's Way* offers a meaningful approach to life that is sublime, eloquent, and inspiring. Reasonable, insightful, and comforting, this book is a true breath of fresh air."

— Phil Zuckerman, PhD, author of *Society without God: What the Least Religious Nations Can Tell Us about Contentment*

"Eric Maisel elevates the tag 'atheist' from a mere denial of the supernatural to a calling — a calling to a high-hearted life of diligence, creativity, and ruthless honesty in maintaining one's integrity in the face of uncaring nature."

— David Cortesi, author of *Secular Wholeness*

"With this book, Eric Maisel does what none of the New Atheists have succeeded in doing: elaborating what atheists *do* believe."

— Hemant Mehta, author of *I Sold My Soul on eBay*

"In *The Atheist's Way*, Eric Maisel takes a giant leap beyond where the New Atheist authors have gone before. Instead of simply criticizing religion or demolishing arguments for the existence of God, Maisel covers new territory and provides a foundation for making meaning and living purposefully without supernatural intervention. A book to be relished by atheists, skeptics, humanists, freethinkers, and unbelievers everywhere."

— Donna Druchunas, Skepchick.org

"I find Eric Maisel's writings more witty than Hitchens, more polished and articulate than Harris, and more informative and entertaining than Dawkins. A five-star read from cover to cover! My only complaint is that Maisel is going to leave the rest of us atheist authors in the dust."

— David Mills, author of *Atheist Universe*

The
Atheist's
Way

ALSO BY ERIC MAISEL

NONFICTION

Affirmations for Artists

Coaching the Artist Within

Creative Recovery

The Creativity Book

Creativity for Life

Deep Writing

Everyday You

Fearless Creating

Fearless Presenting

A Life in the Arts

Living the Writer's Life

Performance Anxiety

Sleep Thinking

Staying Sane in the Arts

Ten Zen Seconds

Toxic Criticism

20 Communication Tips at Work

20 Communication Tips for Families

The Van Gogh Blues

Write Mind

A Writer's Paris

A Writer's San Francisco

A Writer's Space

FICTION

The Blackbirds of Mulhouse

The Black Narc

Dismay

The Fretful Dancer

The Kingston Papers

JOURNALS

Artists Speak

Writers and Artists on Devotion

Writers and Artists on Love

MEDITATION DECKS

Everyday Calm

Everyday Creative

Everyday Smart

E-BOOKS

Becoming a Creativity Coach

The Power of Sleep Thinking

The Atheist's Way

Living Well Without Gods

Eric Maisel

New World Library
Novato, California

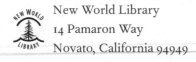

New World Library
14 Pamaron Way
Novato, California 94949

Text design by Tona Pearce Myers

Library of Congress Cataloging-in-Publication Data
Maisel, Eric.
  The atheist's way : living well without gods / Eric Maisel.
    p.   cm.
Includes bibliographical references and index.
ISBN 978-1-57731-642-8 (pbk. : alk. paper)
1. Atheism. 2. Conduct of life. I. Title.
BL2747.3.M296 2009
211'.8—dc22   2008044044

First printing, January 2009
ISBN 978-1-57731-642-8
Printed in the United States on 30% postconsumer-waste recycled paper

New World Library is a proud member of the Green Press Initiative.

10 9 8 7 6 5 4 3 2 1

For Ann

Contents

INTRODUCTION: WE EMBRACE ATHEISM
(For Many Reasons) 1

1. WE HAVE OUR TRADITIONS
(Did You Know That?) 13

2. WE LEAVE OUR CHURCHES
(If We Formerly Believed) 27

3. WE MAKE OUR OWN MEANING
(What a Remarkable Idea!) 43

4. WE INVEST MEANING
(Another Curious Idea!) 55

5. WE NOMINATE OURSELVES
   (As the Heroes of Our Own Stories)   65

6. WE GET BLUE SOMETIMES
   (Who Doesn't?)   79

7. WE DEAL WITH MEANINGLESSNESS
   (Yes, by Making Meaning)   89

8. WE CHOOSE OUR MEANINGS
   (Or Do They Choose Us?)   103

9. WE MAKE IDIOSYNCRATIC MEANING CHOICES
   (As Is Our Right and Obligation)   115

10. WE MAINTAIN MEANING
    (Daily and Over the Long Haul)   127

11. WE MAKE OUR ETHICS
    (As Active Moral Philosophers)   141

12. WE STAND FIRM
    (Even While Consternated)   153

CONCLUSION: WE FIND LIFE AMAZING
   (Exactly as It Is)   165

Notes   177
Index   179
About the Author   187

INTRODUCTION

We Embrace Atheism

(For Many Reasons)

There are no gods (including God). Like all species, ours is a product of nature. This is not something either to celebrate or to mourn. But it can prove a transformational and mind-opening experience to put all gods, religions, and supernatural enthusiasms aside and to explore the world from the point of view of a human being who lives, dies, and is as natural as a tiger or a dove.

You may currently take comfort in gods, religions, and supernatural enthusiasms; or, having cast all that aside, you may feel cold and distraught, as if you were standing alone in the universe. If you are currently taking comfort in gods and religions, I hope that you will find more comfort by living the atheist's way and by replacing those dangerous superstitions with natural beauty. If, having cast all that aside, you are feeling cold and distraught, I hope that this book will provide you with some warmth and relief, for the atheist's way is a rich way, as rich as life itself.

The atheist's way provides you with a complete life plan. You start with the idea that evolution explains you but does not completely dictate to you. Because you are built exactly as you are built, with an instinct for ethics alongside an instinct for self-interest, with a complicated sense of self from which flow your decisions about what self-interest means and what you value (a sense of self that you can modify by applying reason), and with all the other diverse and fascinating aspects of your humanity, you can plot a course that feels righteous and worthy to you.

Living the atheist's way is more than living without gods, religions, and supernatural enthusiasms — much more. It is a way of life that integrates the secular, humanist, scientific, freethinking, skeptical, rationalist, and existential traditions into a complete worldview and that rallies that worldview under the banner of atheism, choosing that precise word as its rallying cry. It chooses *atheism* to make clear that our best chance of survival is for members of our species to grow into a mature view of self-interest, one in which human beings can discuss their conflicting interests without one side betraying the other by playing the god card. That will be a great day, when conflicts can be aired without that card being played.

Most likely it is in your heart to do some good, to manifest your potential, to feel a certain kind of nobility as you face life squarely, to express outrage when you witness injustice, to love another person because the two of you feel drawn to each other, to celebrate human achievements such as freedom of speech, to appreciate beauty and perhaps to create some beauty yourself: the things that constitute a good life. But this good life does not

require conjuring gods, joining religions, or indulging in supernatural enthusiasms. You can have this life by embracing the
atheist's way.

The title of this book suggests that there is (or ought to be)
one and only one atheist's way. Of course that isn't true. Each
atheist's path will differ and must differ, in part because of differences in our nature, in part because of differences in our nur-
ture. What I want the title to communicate is that there can exist
a coherent, comprehensive, righteous, and beautiful way to live
without gods — one that you will have to construct. The atheist's way is *your* way. You will take your journey, and it will not
be identical to my journey.

Atheists feel obliged to think their own thoughts, and so we
are quick to dispute and disagree. Therefore I expect that no one
atheist will agree with the picture I'll be painting in this book.
What I call a "tradition" someone else will call a "thread." What
I call a "choice" someone else will call an "instinct." When I say
that we are obliged to make meaning, many will rise up to call that
idea misleading, unnecessary, dangerous, or, as one of my correspondents dubbed it, "effete." I understand and applaud that
impulse. At the same time, I will be presenting you with some
ideas that I hope you can use as your create your own way.

I am a lifelong atheist. I have never believed in gods or even
come close to believing. If every day people asserted that their
belief in unicorns caused them to wage war on their neighbors,
to hate homosexuals, and to tithe 10 percent of their income to the
unicorn church, and that unicorns accounted for the victory of
their soccer team and the freshness of their sliced bread, you
would feel compelled to stand up and shout, "That is such nonsense!" and, "Those ideas are *so* bad for humanity!" You would

not be railing against unicorns; you would be railing against a certain terrible human practice. I have felt that way about god-talk my whole life: that it is a terrible human practice.

We can do so much better. We can live courageously, we can balance our desires and our immediate self-interest with our sense of duty and our long-term interests, we can decide to sun ourselves and relax or to leap up and work hard at something really difficult, we can play jazz or lend a helping hand, we can stand amazed at life and learn all about it, we can pick ourselves up when we despair, and we can do many different things in a single day, spending one hour relaxing, another hour investigating, another hour loving, another hour creating. Some days will be peaceful; other days we will have to defend ourselves. Some days will pass uneventfully; some days will be filled with drama. This is life, rich and real enough for anyone.

Not only is the atheist way more accurate and more truthful than the god-talk way, but it also confers great advantages. The first is that you feel very free. You are free to think your own thoughts and to have your own feelings. If a passing pastor accuses you of sinning, you feel free to rebuke or ignore him. You know that he has no special knowledge and that he is only betraying your common humanity by quoting gods. You know that no one has any special knowledge about the purpose or lack of purpose of the universe, that there is only scientific knowledge, with its limitations; the speculations of consciousness, with its limitations; and some amount of mystery, shared by us all and quite likely to remain unexplained until the end of time.

This kind of freedom lifts an enormous weight off your shoulders. Freedom is often characterized as a burden and a responsibility, and it is both those things, but it is also a thing of beauty. It is like taking off your heavy overcoat when you get indoors or having your shackles removed when you get off the chain gang. You are free to sit in the sun for an hour without feeling guilty. You are free to cut off contact with toxic people and to eliminate toxic beliefs from your system. You are free to create stresses and strains in service to a task that you value, whether that task is writing a novel, starting a nonprofit, politicking for a candidate, or intervening in your child's life. You are free to step out of the cultural trance, to step off a cliff and hang glide, or to step to one side and let someone else win. You are as free as you can be — that is, as free as nature allows.

The word *atheist* is a larger, friendlier, and more glorious word than you might imagine. It stands for a conviction about the nonexistence of gods, but it represents other things as well. It is about a solidarity with nature and with the universe: we are not afraid of the universe in which we live, we do not create dragons and devils with which to scare ourselves, we are not frightened that a vacuum is empty or that we begin dying as soon as we are born. We are exactly, precisely, and wholly natural. We are human beings, with enough fascinating attributes to make even the most incurious among us stand up and take notice. To say *human being* is to say plenty: and that plenty is what the word *atheist* connotes.

IF YOU CURRENTLY BELIEVE

There are so many believers with good hearts! But that doesn't make their belief systems any less faulty or, ultimately, dangerous. If you are a believer who is currently content to remain faithful to your Catholic, Hindu, Protestant, Jewish, or Muslim beliefs because you have a circle of friends, a social network, and a whole life built around that religion, because you reckon that you can do good work and be a good person just as well inside your religion as outside it, and because you see no particular reason to leave your religion, even though aspects of it strike you as false, I would like you to consider the possibility that you have made the wrong investment. You really might prefer living the atheist's way. It is truer to reality and it frees you up enormously. In one fell swoop you could leave a lot of humbug behind you.

I offer you this same invitation if you participate in one of the "river" religions. Some religions, such as Buddhism and Taoism, do not posit the existence of gods. I am calling these disparate religions river religions to distinguish them from god-based religions and to catch something of their flavor. The river religions tend to posit an indivisible reality flowing eternally. At first glance this view of life does not seem too incompatible with the atheist's way. The river religions can be very attractive to people who do not believe in bearded gods dictating to humankind. But they are no less false than the god-based religions, because ultimately they are dogmatic and create an unnecessary wall between a person and reality.

And what about an enthusiasm for Wicca, paganism, past lives, psychic powers, remote viewing, spoon bending, astrology, Tarot, the I Ching, palm reading, haunted houses, sacred sites, vampires, séances, and a thousand other variations of new age, paranormal, and supernatural belief? These too interfere with your ability to assess well, to choose well, and to live well, and therefore they ought to be discarded. Like the god religions and the river religions, our supernatural enthusiasms have their undeniable seductive side, their psychological pull, and their blandishments. But they don't serve you any better than god-talk or river-talk. Believing in them, investing time and energy in them, and imbibing in their metaphoric power diminish you. The more you consult your chart, the more personal power you relinquish; the more you identify a site as "sacred," the less real you make your life.

The god religions, the river religions, and the world of supernatural enthusiasms do not serve you. They force you to rein in your intelligence, they make claims that you do not honestly believe, they smell of illegitimate shortcut, and they hurt your chances of taking a fearless inventory of your beliefs and charting a course that will make you proud.

Even if you currently believe, I hope that you will read these chapters. If you do, you will hear from believers like you who made the journey from belief to atheism. You will hear why they made that change and how they are faring. You will learn that the atheist tradition is a very long and honorable one, thousands of years old, exactly as old as your religion — if not older. You will learn that your belief system does not relieve you of the responsibility for making thoughtful rather than dogmatic choices — that, in this regard, you and atheists are in exactly the same boat. I think that you will learn many things of interest to you, so I invite you to come along for the ride.

THE ECSTASY OF PARTICIPATION

At some point in our lives, most of us have speculated that the universe is pointless, purposeless, or meaningless. But what do we mean by this? We aren't saying that it doesn't have order. We are saying that the universe is a different sort of thing from a human being — that it is inhuman. It doesn't have thoughts or feelings, it can't pay attention, it can't put on its socks, and it can't mourn a loss by its hometown team (or have a hometown team). That is what is in our hearts when we conclude that the universe is meaningless. We don't doubt that it has order, but we recognize that it is not our parent, our sponsor, or our caretaker.

In short, it doesn't care, and that can bring a person down. Believers or atheists, we are quite likely to think, "Isn't it ridiculous that an ice-cold universe creates this sentient passing speck — me — and then forces me to deal with indignities like toothaches and an extra thirty pounds?" We get blue, and that blueness can become our default feeling about life, a feeling that is never very far from spilling over and turning into grief. We get a speeding ticket or fail at a task and we go to a sad place, a place that has nothing to do with that speeding ticket or that failed task and everything to do with our wonder about why we are even bothering.

Any modern person, believer or atheist, can feel this way. The believer, to take some comfort and to find some solace, allows his brain to perpetrate a trick that it is quite willing to play: to conjure a god and a more pleasant universe. So he turns to religion, even if to find that solace he must ignore his religion's monstrous contradictions, swallow his doubts, smile at ludicrous claims, and accept that he has transformed a metaphor into a pseudo-reality. Before the advent of modern science and the last four hundred years of increased knowledge, believers may have believed in some seamless way, uninterrupted by doubts. Now every sensible, educated, modern believer knows in a corner of consciousness that she is buying her solace on the cheap — she *knows* that the pope is not infallible, that god did not give the Jews a piece of land, that there is nothing like nirvana, and so on. So she bites her tongue and tries to get as much out of her religion as she can, covering her eyes to all the rest — and not really dealing with the central issue of cosmic indifference.

The contemporary believer suffers from her version of existential angst; so does the contemporary atheist. The atheist endeavors to finds warmth, solace, and purpose in human engagements such as family, love, learning, good deeds, sex, entertainment, and so on, and he often does find fine solace in these activities. He may keep himself very busy, amused, and interested as a trial lawyer, biologist, corporate executive, high-tech worker, or another professional whose days are filled with activity and whose evenings are filled with good meals and fine wine. But even in the midst of this excellent life, many an atheist is burdened by the feeling that she and her efforts do not "really" matter. The thought that she is a disposable throwaway in a meaningless universe can wreak havoc just beneath the surface, draining her of motivational energy and setting her up for a depression.

Both the disgruntled believer and the mourning atheist can move to a better place by making some new calculations and decisions and by announcing that life is an eloquent project ripe for passionate undertaking. You let go of wondering what the universe wants of you, you let go of the fear that nothing matters, and you announce that you will make life mean exactly what you intend it to mean. This is an amazing, glorious, and triumphant announcement, and it rights your ship — for all time, if you keep repeating the announcement.

We are on the threshold of understanding a shining idea: that each life can have meaning, even if the universe has none. This nature has granted us. I get to decide what will make me feel righteous and happy, and you get to decide what will make you feel righteous and happy. You can turn the meaning that was waiting to be made into the meaning of your life. By announcing your intentions to yourself, by making the requisite effort, and by manifesting the courage that is part of your inheritance, you aim yourself in a brilliant direction: the direction of your own creation.

Our species needs you to do this. Consider the following mind experiment. Let's say that in each generation a majority of people define self-interest in a narrow way and back their church, club, company, and country; produce lots of offspring; grab scarce resources; pad their bank accounts; and try as best they can to keep others from sharing in the global pie. At the same time, a small minority defines self-interest another way and strives to defend some humanist principles, advance civilization, help the weak, promote sharing, and so on. What will happen?

What will happen is that there will be many important advances, owing to that small minority, but the selfish efforts of the vast majority will threaten to swamp those advances and return our fragile civilization to an ice age. Isn't that exactly the scenario we are facing? We need real warriors who define self-interest in a way that favors civilization, since so many of our fellow human beings are defining self-interest more selfishly and threatening us all. We need atheist-warriors on the side of the species who, having thought it through, decide to side with the good and fight for the future.

Let me remind you why I am framing these ideas around the term *atheism* and not around some less charged word such as *secularism, humanism, rationalism, skepticism, naturalism, existentialism,* or *freethinking.* First, it would be a shame to miss what may be an opportunity, since we are perhaps finally ready to face an indifferent universe with new views and to live purposefully and well without gods. Second, rallying around atheism underscores the heightened threat that religious belief poses to the survival of the species. It was one thing for human beings of another age to use god-talk to justify inquisitions. But the world has changed. Now we have nuclear weapons and a thousand other ways to kill each other. We need atheism to grow as a movement because we need to remove the god card from the hands of the selfishly self-interested. For thousands of years smart men and women have been saying the same thing: here we are; now let us make the best of it. Against these few voices billions of other voices have been marshaled in support of gods and the supernatural. The reasons for this are obvious enough. Religion is excellent cover for the unscrupulous; it is much harder to think than it is to pray; if you are born into a religion, you have to fend off your parents and your neighbors to get free of it; it is comforting; it makes you feel select and knowledgeable; admitting that you don't know requires courage; and so on.

Perhaps we are now ready for a multitude to join those previously scarce atheist voices. The atheist's way is a beautiful way, a truthful way, and it may very well prove to be the only way for our species to have a fighting chance for survival. The exact way you choose to be an atheist is for you to determine. In the following chapters, I will outline what that way might include and how you might design it. In the end, you will decide for yourself and adopt the way that is completely your own.

CHAPTER ONE

We Have
Our Traditions

(Did You Know That?)

M any people are not aware that the tradition of atheism is as
old as that of the world's religions. One of the lures of religion is the way that it plays on our unconscious belief that "old
things" must also be "good things." For that reason, we need to
recognize and understand that atheism is "old" too. As far back
as thousands of years ago, sensible people like you and me were
seeing through religion. These were often the best and the bright-
est of their era — thinkers and creators we still revere for their
insights and their works.

You may prefer to call this a "thread" rather than a "tradition," if the word *tradition* connotes something too systematic,
codified, or ritualized for you. Yet the point remains the same:
individuals have been voicing atheist views for thousands of
years, even when doing so could have cost them their lives. If
you've always thought that atheism is a new philosophy arising

only as recently as the Age of Enlightenment or with the Industrial Revolution, then listen to these Greek, Roman, Chinese, and Arab voices from thousands of years ago:

Heraclitus (c. 535–475 BCE): "Religion is a disease."

Aristophanes (448–380 BCE): "Surely you don't believe in the gods. What's your argument? Where's your proof?"

Petronius Arbiter (c. 27–66 CE): "It was fear that first brought gods into the world."

Seneca (4 BCE–65 CE): "Religion is regarded by the common people as true, by the wise as false, and by the rulers as useful."

Abu al-Ahmad (973–1057 CE): "The world holds two classes of men — intelligent men without religion and religious men without intelligence."

Cicero (106–43 BCE): "What old woman is so stupid now as to tremble at those tales of hell which were once so firmly believed in?"

Epicurus (341–270 BCE): "Faith is the credulous belief in the reality of phantoms."

Confucius (551 BCE–479 BCE): "Why talk of spirits when you do not understand men?"

Pliny the Elder (23–79 CE): "It is ridiculous to suppose that the great head of things, whatever it may be, pays any regard to human affairs."

Aristotle (384–322 BCE): "Men create gods in their own image."

Atheism is a partner to the freethinking tradition, the rationalist tradition, the naturalist tradition, the secular humanist tradition, and the scientific tradition. It is also a partner to the existential tradition: the tradition of lone individuals experiencing their subjectivity, fallibility, freedom, and mortality. And it is a partner to the truth-telling tradition: the tradition that remarks on the emperor's nakedness, the indecency of tyranny, and the corruption that comes with power. Likewise, it is a partner to the tradition of martyrdom: the tradition of brave individuals sacrificing their lives because they refuse to renounce their convictions.

Even within the world's religions, freethinking threads have existed since the beginning. This is naturally most true in those religions that do not posit the existence of gods, such as Buddhism, Taoism, and Confucianism. But it is a feature of all religions. Many religious thinkers have argued that it is incumbent on believers to reason clearly, act honorably, and take responsibility for their actions. If you are a believer and don't want to abandon your religious beliefs quite yet, there is still ample reason for you to decide to take responsibility for your actions and to reject religious dogma that makes no sense to you.

Teachers in each of the religious traditions have argued that engaging in the rituals and trappings of religion is no substitute for doing the right thing and taking responsibility. Listen to these three more modern speakers, one a Catholic, one a Protestant, and one a Jew:

Thomas Aquinas (thirteenth-century theologian and philosopher): "The highest manifestation of life consists in this: that a being governs its own actions. A thing that is always subject to the direction of another is somewhat of a dead thing."

Geoffrey Fisher (archbishop of Canterbury from 1945 to 1961): "There is a sacred realm of privacy for every man and woman where he makes his choices and decisions, a realm of his own essential rights and liberties."

Martin Buber (twentieth-century Hasidic scholar): "Infinity shall be contained in every deed of man, in his speaking and seeing, listening and walking, standing still and lying down. In order to perfect oneself, one must renew oneself day by day."

Each of these believers articulates the demand that his fellow believers thoughtfully and actively participate in their own lives. Not only must you not shirk from doing the work of life; you must figure out what that work is. Even if a god has a plan for you, you are not privy to that plan, so you must operate as if you and you alone are constructing the plan of your life. Those whispers and signs you are waiting for may simply be the result of hallucinations or indigestion.

These religious existential speakers are arguing that you must think through how you want to be good, productive, and righteous, trusting that your god's hand is on your shoulder as you make your own choices. If you do not embrace the idea that you must take responsibility for your beliefs, your decisions, and your moral direction, and if you act as a follower rather than a leader, you make the world a safer place for pious selfishness and pure humbug. They are defining life as a project that demands your best efforts and your considered intentions, an admonition not unlike the one that existentialists make.

It is written in the Koran:

God does not compel a soul
To do what is beyond its capacity:

It gets what it has earned,
And is responsible for what it deserves.

In other words, the believer must take responsibility for his actions. He cannot use a divine presence as an excuse or a scapegoat. He must earn his righteousness, and he must think through, and then take responsibility for, his choices. This passage also addresses the objection that taking responsibility for being righteous and good is simply too much work. The Koran articulates great faith in the individual, assuring each one of the faithful that he is capable of ascertaining what constitutes ethical action and then following through on his considered opinions.

The Koran also makes it explicit that when you refuse to take responsibility and when you fail to act ethically, you are not permitted to turn around and complain, "Well, I followed someone I thought was a holy man." You are not permitted to fall back on the argument that something was demanded of you by this book or that leader. You are simply not permitted the tactic of refusing to think through what are the right, proper, and humane things for you to do.

In the Hindu tradition, Ramakrishna (1836–1886) explained, "Let each man follow his own path. If he sincerely and ardently wishes to know God, peace be unto him! He will surely reach Him."[1] Ramakrishna, a teacher who according to Hindu tradition attained enlightenment, plainly announces that you must make your own decisions about your path. In answer to the question always posed to atheists, "Well, if I am forced to make my own decisions, what if I decide to kick puppies or rob old ladies?" again Ramakrishna is clear: you will not do this, and all will be well "if you sincerely and ardently wish to know God." If you engage your moral sense, all will be well.

In the Buddhist tradition, the following teaching of the Buddha is telling: "Yes, Kalamas, it is proper that you have doubt, that you have perplexity, for a doubt has arisen in a matter which is doubtful. Now, look you Kalamas, do not be led by reports, or tradition, or hearsay. . . . But when you know for yourself that certain things are unwholesome and wrong, and bad, then give them up . . . and when you know for yourself that certain things are wholesome and good, then accept them and follow them."[2]

The Buddha puts it simply and clearly: you must decide for yourself what will constitute a good, righteous life for you; and then you must commit to what you have decided. The work you choose will not be beyond you; according to the Koran, you have been given the capacity to follow through on your commitments. Nor should you be afraid of taking a wrong step; as Ramakrishna put it, any path has the potential to be the right path, as long as you are aiming for the "high." Yes, you will be uncertain at times. Yes, there will be moments when you need to reevaluate your choices. But you must have faith that what you choose for yourself is right for you and that you have the ability to accomplish the arduous work of authentic living.

Nowhere is this existential note more beautifully heard than in the words of the Taoist poets. Listen to this poem, for example, by Juan Chi (210–263 CE):

POEM OF MY HEART

Twelve o'clock.
Unable to sleep.
I get up and sit,
I play and sing to the ch'in.

The fragile cloths
    mirror a brilliant moon;
Metallic wind
    agitates my sleeve.
One single crane
    cries past the farthest fields;
Another bird
    sings in the northward grove.
Go back, go forth.
    What shall any of us find?
Sorrowful thoughts.
    Solitude. Shaken nerve.

Or to this one, by Kuo P'u (276–324 CE), which sounds like an existential battle cry:

"TZU YEH" SONG

Let others find themselves alike,
My will is obstinately I.
My winter blinds are wide to winds
And long, in cold,
my curtains fly.[3]

Side by side with these existential voices speaking from within the world's religions are the voices of those who refused to accept the blandishments of faith and who, for thousands of years, even through the Dark Ages, stood up for their atheist beliefs. Most of these martyrs are unknown to us, their history erased by their oppressors. Their very absence from the historical record is an eloquent feature of our tradition.

A few of these lone individuals managed to be heard and are remembered by Joseph McCabe in his book *A Biographical Dictionary of Ancient, Medieval and Modern Freethinkers*.[4] There was the Roman orator Dio Chrysostom (c. 40–120 CE), known as "Dio of the Golden Mouth," who denounced slavery a thousand years before any Christian leader thought to do so. There was Aurelius Celsus, a second-century opponent of the church, who mercilessly satirized the gospel story of Jesus. There was Domitius Ulpianus (d. 228 CE), a Roman jurist who, from 211 to 222 CE, humanized Roman law and appealed to the "laws of nature" as his authority. There was Muavia (510–585 CE), the first Syrian caliph, whose parents bitterly denounced Muhammad as an impostor and who moved his people from barbarism to civilization in a single generation.

There was John Scotus Erigena (810–877 CE), an Irish philosopher several times condemned by the church for arguing that "reason preceded faith." There was Tai-tsung, Chinese emperor of the Tang dynasty from 762 to 779 CE, an avowed atheist who preached tolerance and whose reign has been described as one of "unrivalled brilliance and glory" and about whom it was said, "No ruler of any country has had sounder claims to be entitled Great." There was the German emperor Frederick II (1194–1250 CE), "the Wonder of the World," a freethinker whose stance was so well-known that when a book about Moses, Jesus, and Muhammad called *The Three Impostors* appeared, he received the attribution.

There was Francesco d'Ascoli (known as Cecco) (1257–1327 CE), scientist and professor at Bologna University, "a man of immense erudition and great ability burned at the stake for his freethinking and plain speaking."[5] There was the Italian humanist Lorenzo Valla (1407–1457 CE), an atheist who, as secretary to the king of Naples, exposed forged documents used by the papacy to perpetrate a famous fraud. There was Michael Servetus (1511–1553 CE), who rejected the doctrine of the Trinity, was driven out of Spain, took up medicine in France, and, while passing through Switzerland, was arrested by Calvin and burned at the stake.

And there was the great freethinking Persian astronomer and poet Omar Khayyám (c. 1048–1122 CE). Listen to a few verses from *The Rubaiyat*, a poem that its best-known translator, the English poet Edward Fitzgerald, had to have printed anonymously, since blasphemy was a serious crime in Victorian England:

Why, all the saints and sages who discussed
Of the two worlds so learnedly, are thrust
Like foolish prophets forth; their words to scorn
Are scattered, and their mouths are stopped with dust.

Oh, threats of hell and hopes of paradise!
One thing at least is certain — this life flies;
One thing is certain, and the rest is lies;
The flower that once has blown forever dies.

And that inverted bowl we call the sky
Whereunder crawling coop'd we live and die
Lift not your hands to it for help — for it
Rolls impotently on as thou and I.

The revelations of the devout and learned
Who rose before us and as prophets burned
Are all but stories, which, awoke from sleep
They told their comrades, and to sleep returned.[6]

There are thousands of beautiful, important quotations from our tradition that I would love to share with you, if only there were space. So I will limit myself to just five from each of four different centuries:

FROM THE SEVENTEENTH CENTURY

Pierre Bayle (1647–1706): "No nations are more warlike than those which profess Christianity."

Sir Francis Bacon (1561–1626): "In every age, natural philosophy had a troublesome adversary; namely superstition and the blind and immoderate zeal of religion."

Giordano Bruno (1548–1600): "Nothing appears to be really durable, eternal and worthy of the name of principle, save matter alone."

Ben Jonson (1572–1637): "What excellent fools religion makes of men."

Thomas Hobbes (1588–1679): "Theology is the kingdom of darkness."

FROM THE EIGHTEENTH CENTURY

Edward Gibbon (1737–1794): "The practice of superstition is so congenial to the multitude that, if they are forcibly awakened, they still regret the loss of their pleasing vision. So urgent on the vulgar is the necessity of believing, that the fall of any system of mythology will probably be succeeded by the introduction of some other mode of superstition."

Denis Diderot (1713–1784): "Men will never be free until the last king is strangled in the entrails of the last priest."

David Hume (1711–1776): "Examine the religious principles which have, in fact, prevailed in the world, and you will scarcely believe that they are anything but sick men's dreams."

Voltaire (1694–1778): "On religion, many are destined to reason wrongly; others not to reason at all; and others to persecute those who do reason."

Henry Fielding (1707–1754): "No man has ever sat down calmly unbiased to reason out his religion and not ended by rejecting it."

FROM THE NINETEENTH CENTURY

Percy Bysshe Shelley (1792–1822): "Every time that we say that God is the author of some phenomenon, that signifies that we are ignorant of how such a phenomenon was caused by the forces of nature."

Ralph Waldo Emerson (1803–1882): "As men's prayers are a disease of the will, so are their creeds a disease of the intellect."

John Stuart Mill (1806–1873): "God is a word to express, not our ideas, but our want of them."

Abraham Lincoln (1809–1865): "It will not do to investigate the subject of religion too closely, as it is apt to lead to infidelity."

Elizabeth Cady Stanton (1815–1902): "The religious superstitions of women perpetuate their bondage more than all other adverse influences."

Thomas Alva Edison (1847–1931): "Nature made us — nature did it all — not the gods of the religions. Religion is all bunk and all bibles are man-made."

W. E. B. Du Bois (1868–1963): "My religious development has been slow and uncertain but eventually I became a freethinker and from my thirtieth year on I have increasingly regarded the church as an institution which defended such evils as slavery, color caste, exploitation of labor, and war."

Albert Einstein (1879–1955): "I cannot imagine a God who rewards and punishes the objects of his creation, whose purposes are modeled after our own — a God, in short, who is but a reflection of human frailty. Neither can I believe that the individual survives the death of his body, although feeble souls harbor such thoughts through fear or ridiculous egotism."

Ayn Rand (1905–1982): "Religion is the first enemy of the ability to think. This ability is not used by men to one-tenth of its possibility, yet before they learn to think they are discouraged by being ordered to take things on faith. Faith is the worst curse of mankind, as the exact antithesis and enemy of thought."

Anthony Storr (1920–2001): "What chiefly concerns and alarms many of us are the problems arising from religious

fanaticism. As long as large numbers of militant enthu-
siasts are persuaded that they alone have the truth, and
that the rest of us are infidels, we remain under threat."

I hope that you will delve deeply into our tradition. If you are
a doubting believer, examining our tradition will help you come
over to reason, responsibility, and the atheist's way. If you are an
atheist, reading about our fine tradition will remind you that you
are not alone and will provide you with excellent material for your
debates and celebrations.

CHAPTER TWO

We Leave
Our Churches

(If We Formerly Believed)

Not only do we have a beautiful freethinking, antireligious, antihumbug, atheistic tradition to learn from and appreciate, but we also have the powerful "conversion" stories of former believers who now embrace atheism. I am a lifelong atheist, but millions of atheists started out believing. In this chapter I want to share eight of their stories. These eloquent accounts paint a picture of the journey from belief to atheism and the rewards of arriving at that destination. Better than polemical fireworks and fine arguments, these accounts may inspire you to make that journey yourself.

MARCIA'S STORY

I remember being in my early teens, sitting in church with my little hat and my white gloves (don't laugh; this was the fifties in

Alabama), being perfectly aware that everybody was eying each other's clothes and thinking about what snide things they were going to say about somebody afterward and how they weren't listening to what the preacher was saying (but neither was I). I was also thinking that what the preacher was really there for was to raise money, not even mainly to do anything for God, or to help people, just to raise money for the building fund. And resenting the heck out of *having* to put 10 percent of my allowance or whatever I had earned into that collection plate or God would be disappointed in me.

The process of moving from believer to nonbeliever took a while, and I don't remember it being particularly traumatic. It just happened. I changed. I was a believer, and I wanted to be baptized, but I waited until I was twelve to do that because I understood from somewhere inside me that I should wait until the age of responsibility. The real change started when I was thirteen or fourteen and first read about comparative religions, having never before fully realized there *was* any other religion.

Everybody in my world was either Baptist or Methodist, with a few Presbyterians. If I stayed a Saturday night with a Methodist or Presbyterian friend, I would go to church Sunday morning with them, having no problem with that. No other religion was real to me except in the sense of having to contribute to the fund to help save the heathens in Korea or China. But in my readings, I saw that the world's religions were all rooted in the same human needs of helplessness and the desire for a protector and were great tools for whatever leader arose to use to gather his clan around for whatever task was at hand.

By the time I finished college, I had gone from believing that everything was either black or white, either this was a sin or it wasn't, to realizing that many, many things were neither black nor white, or were both black and white, and that most things were shades of gray. And that whatever "thing" there was that we as a human race considered "God" in all its historical forms and shapes, that thing might or might not be there, either. In the forty-plus years since then, I haven't changed much in my thinking, except that I've quit worrying about whether the God "thing" is there or not. I haven't met it myself, if it is there, and so I mistrust those who say they have.

The easiest part has been getting on with life without worrying about whether I was doing what God would want me to do, without worrying about whether my church and family would approve of me. The hardest part has been shaping my own way through a life lived in the dichotomy of trying to do and be what I think people should do and be while having "everything" opened up as a possibility with no church dogma to guide me. The other really hard part has been dealing with my parents, not just when I first said I was not a believer, but forever after that, especially when my mother was dying of cancer and wanted me to pray with her. She was more worried about godless me than about herself. Since I didn't want to cause her any more pain, I kept my mouth shut and did what she wanted me to do.

What remains hard is the lack of community and not having a "church home," which may not be comprehensible to atheists who didn't grow up in one. There's just a hole there in my life, and no group of friends with shared interests fills that hole. I guess it's really from lacking the certainty and security of *knowing* I have the answer and that God is going to take care of me, which I grew up with as my foundation. But I am still better off with these difficulties than trying to believe in something that I know doesn't exist.

ROBERT'S STORY

I accepted Jesus when I was seventeen and a senior in high school after living a mostly agnostic, non-Christian life. I became born-again, under the influence of friends and as the result of a Bible study class I attended. I plunged myself into the Christian lifestyle and belief system and ended up attending and graduating from a conservative Christian liberal arts college. Though I remained a practicing believer until about the age of twenty-four, the seeds of my deconversion had always been present. I always considered myself a rational thinker and an advocate of science. Somehow I was able to suppress that mind-set for the seven or so years I remained a faithful Christian.

Two things led to my deconversion. First were the creeping but ever-present doubts about the inerrancy of Scripture (and from that, the whole of my Christian worldview slowly crumbled). Second was my increased interest in and self-education about science. That drove the final nail in the coffin. In particular, I think, was my dissatisfaction with the creationist tendency to play fast and loose with the facts and the twisted reasoning required to maintain a biblical commitment to creation.

The hardest part, I think, was making the break with the thought patterns and habits of rationalization that come so naturally to Christians and other religious adherents. This was made somewhat easier for me since I was in the process of making several geographic moves after college and graduate school, so I was removed from the influence of my friends and fellow churchgoers. I spent time exploring some more liberal churches but eventually gave in to my inner atheist and left it all behind.

The easiest part was finally being able to embrace what I felt I secretly had known all the time: that the stories of the Bible were really myths and that I no longer had any reason to try to justify belief in the impossible, the highly improbable, or the absurd. I was finally free to embrace and express my skepticism and rational thinking. What remains hard? Only the occasional encounters with old friends from my "previous life" who now view me as a backslider or a heretic. Borrowing from the AA model, I primarily think of myself as a "recovering Christian."

BARBARA'S STORY

I was about twelve when I stopped believing. My religious education and experience had mostly consisted of attending Sunday school regularly for many years and having read and reread a set of *Bible Stories for Children* books that my parents had bought for me. What precipitated the change for me, oddly enough, was reading a book about UFOs. I guess as such things go, it was probably a moderately reasonable and noncrazy example of the UFO literature. There was a (in retrospect, quite scientifically accurate) chapter that talked about the likelihood of life having arisen on other planets, in the context of how it was thought that life first arose on earth. There was a discussion of self-replicating molecules and evolution, and of experiments in which primitive terrane conditions were replicated in laboratories and gave rise to slightly more complex organic molecules in ways that were at least suggestive.

I'd always been very interested in various scientific subjects. I already had a general grasp of the scientific method and how it worked, and I had accepted it as pretty obvious that science was a good way of finding out about things. But I had also been told by the many authoritative adults in my life that God created life on earth, in the fashion outlined in Genesis, and I had accepted this as the simple truth. I immediately grasped the fact that these things could not both be true, and as soon as I started thinking about it, it seemed to me quite obvious that the only reason I believed in God or anything in the Bible at all was because I had been told to. And if it was a question of choosing between what I had been told and actual "evidence," there was no question at all.

When my Sunday school teacher informed me that science was fine just so long as it didn't conflict with the Bible, that pretty much clinched it for me, because that made no sense to me at all. If science is a good way of discovering the truth, well, then it's a good way of discovering the truth. Right? And there's no reason to arbitrarily wall things off from it, or to declare swatches of it automatically invalid based on ... what? Based on nothing at all, really, just on stories. So that was it for me.

The hardest part of the process was the terrible sense of betrayal and shame I felt, betrayal because my parents and teachers had "lied" to me all those years and I had blindly trusted them. And shame partly for having fallen for it — you'd think I'd know better after that whole Santa Claus thing — but mostly because, irrationally, I felt that turning my back on Christianity made me a bad, disobedient kid. And I knew that the shame was irrational, which led to anger at religious traditions and at the world in general. I also felt sort of hypocritical, because I'd been very enthusiastic about all those Bible stories, and the result was that I didn't feel that I could talk to anybody about it, that it was something I had to hide.

I was able to tell my parents that I didn't want to go to Sunday school anymore, but I could not bring myself to tell them why, even though, looking back, I'm quite sure my mother, at least, would have been fine with it. But then, she never talked much about being an agnostic, and I never realized the word even applied to her until many, many years later. Also hard was when, after my parents' divorce, my dad converted to a particularly straitlaced brand of fundamentalism, and I found that, given that I couldn't bring myself to talk about religion, I pretty much couldn't hold a conversation with him at all.

Converting from belief to unbelief in itself was incredibly easy. It was obvious to me as soon as I started thinking about it critically which side of the faith-versus-evidence issue I was on. It was troubling emotionally, for the reasons mentioned above, but it wasn't an intellectual struggle at all. Sometimes the social awkwardness and the difficulty of not getting overly emotional and angry about the whole matter is still hard for me, but at least it's a heck of a lot easier than it was when I was thirteen!

ALAN'S STORY

I became a Buddhist in my late teens as a way to stabilize my life. I was already drinking heavily — my family was littered with alcoholics, and I could see where I was heading. It is something of a miracle that I didn't head directly to alcoholism without passing go, because my teens were a crazy, terrible time of confusion, isolation, and family turmoil. But for some reason I didn't want to give up on myself and become like my parents, so I started hanging out at the Zen center when I was seventeen or eighteen and really got into Buddhism. By the time I was twenty I could do even the most rigorous retreat — the seven-day ones with no talking and a zillion hours of sitting meditation — without batting an eyelash.

Slowly, though, I became disenchanted. Part of it was that our leaders acted pretty scandalously. Our roshi had a reputation for groping women, and there were a lot of discrepancies between professed morality and the actual behavior of the people around me. But I don't think that their bad behaviors or hypocrisy shook my belief in Zen Buddhism. There's no particular reason to expect practitioners of any religion to be anything but human. What shook me was the feeling that everyone I knew at the Zen center was seriously depressed. All the sitting, all the silence, all the detachment, all the self-control seemed to lead to such a lack of exuberance that I began to wonder, is depression built into this way? If so, why bother with it?

That's when it struck me that Buddhism was no larger or more light filled a philosophy than the religions with gods. All its tenets had a kind of antilife and anti-intellectual feel to them. Why was it such a virtue to just peel a potato when peeling a potato, rather than peeling that potato while also dreaming about some fabulous story you might write or some exciting woman you might meet? Why such a stringent focus on asceticism, discipline, and detachment when life cried out to be lived? Why so many koan riddles and jokes and tricks, which only supported the idea of hierarchical knowing? And why the concern with lineages and the rivalries and the bad blood between Zen masters? It actually all stopped making sense.

It is not such a long way from Buddhism to atheism, and yet it is a vast distance, because you are giving up a system of knowing, with all the comforts that come with gongs and chimes and incense and singing bowls, for personal knowing, with all the doubts and fears that come with self-reliance. Probably I needed that structure and support through my teens and into my mid-twenties, during a time when I might have fallen completely apart without my Zen center "family." But I outgrew that family and had to leave the security of that home: something, it seems to me, that every adult is obliged to do.

JANET'S STORY

I believed as a child. My family was not particularly religious. My mother believed in a god, but she didn't see any reason to go to church. She felt she could pray or worship in her own home in her own way. My oldest sister sometimes took me to Sunday school while she went to church. I believed because it never occurred to me not to. It was simply something I had grown up with.

I was preoccupied with other things and didn't really make much of an effort to look at this "higher power" until I was fully an adult. Over time I started to believe in a more generic type of higher power, a "force" for good, rather than in any kind of being. Then for many years I labeled myself an agnostic, meaning, really, that I had not found the religion or higher power idea that really suited me. It was not until perhaps the last ten or fifteen years (I am now sixty-one) that I really looked at belief. It is one thing to look at religions and realize how bizarre they are, but quite another to look at this concept of a higher power. Like many in my generation I was open to the concept of a different way of communicating (telepathy?) or a way for the dead to stick around with no bodies. Once I started putting my mind to thinking about this higher power I found that I was moving into the atheist camp, yet I was still "not sure."

Gaining a greater understanding of evolution tipped the scales. When I understood just how it all could happen without divine intervention and how everything can ultimately be explained, how there is no reason to call on some strange other type of natural law, I was all the way there. This all happened so gradually that I can't pinpoint any turning points, except for my reading of Richard Dawkins's *The Blind Watchmaker*.[1] That book made so much sense to me that it brought it all together. There has really been no hard part to the transition — except dealing with people who are still being led around by their beliefs.

LAURA'S STORY

It took me about ten years to let go of believing, and it was quite a painful process. It was painful in part because my mother stopped communicating with me (again) when she caught me reading a book about Jesus — and that was back at the beginning of the process when I still believed and was just trying to learn more. She thought that reading about Jesus meant that I didn't have enough of the right kind of faith and didn't "have Jesus in my heart." She and I already had a strained relationship, and any time I didn't believe whatever she wanted me to believe or follow whatever she wanted me to follow, she withdrew. Daring to read a book was just the straw that broke the camel's back.

It was painful to realize that both society and, to a large degree, my life, were based on a lie and on false beliefs. It was painful to let go of that old system of thinking about the world and to build a new foundation based on evidence. Everything in our culture is geared to support and promote the idea of supernatural forces — gods, ghosts, spirits, ESP, psychics, astrology, astral projection, angels, demons, heaven, hell, even vampires, zombies, werewolves, elves: our literature is filled with these things. Some of it is easy to let go of, and some of it runs deeper and is much harder to eradicate. It's tremendously hard to throw that all off when we're surrounded by supernatural stories everywhere we look.

For me, it was a slow process that involved a lot of research and study and books and thinking and journaling. One thing that made the process easier was finding online groups, books, and well-known experts who had blazed the atheist path before me and could provide maps and information about skepticism, critical thinking, science, and all the other rational tools that we need. Once I found the rational path, it was just a matter of time before I accepted the label *atheist* and completely let go of the old beliefs. I now belong to a local secular humanist group and attend their meetings and update their website.

What remains hard is the knowledge that if I tell people openly that I'm an atheist I'm likely to be rejected. It doesn't bother me to be respectful of other people's religious rituals when I need to be, like remaining silent through holiday prayers. But I refuse to listen to any attempt at converting me and will contradict anyone who directly tells me anything like "you can't argue with faith." I don't hide my atheism, and I don't often advertise it either, but I am very clear about what I simply will no longer tolerate.

DANNY'S STORY

I grew up in a second-generation Chinese American household with a huge extended family of scores of cousins and a belief system that was part Taoist, part Confucian, part cultural Chinese, and — the biggest part — part pure superstition. There was no unverified, crazy thing that someone didn't believe in, whether it was the absolute sway that numerology held over human events, the merits of this or that herbal remedy or bizarre concoction, or how a sideways glance or a brazen look might ruin your whole family.

The way that folks in my family could make arbitrary, iron-clad laws out of pure superstition made me want to scream. But for years and years I held it all in and attended to my homework and my duties like a good son, preparing myself to "make it" in the American culture and to live the American dream. I did just that, getting a business degree from a good college and going straight into a high-paying, high-pressure job that kept me jumping all week long. But that began wearing me down, emotionally and physically, and I started pining for something — I couldn't really say what. So I threw myself into Taoism.

I read the primary texts and the commentaries, I tried to make sense of ideas like yin and yang and "the Way," I attended lectures, I wrote in my journal about my "spiritual adventure," I even wrote Taoist poetry about crystalline nights and the mournful sounds of distant foghorns. I don't know if I wanted a religion, a philosophy, or what, but I spent several years making investigations, pilgrimages, and a real effort, even as I pursued the American dream with all my energy. Probably I thought that I needed some spiritual antidote to my secular immersion in business; no doubt that's why I kept at my Taoist pursuits. But finally it fell apart — I saw right through it. There was nothing there but air and superstition and, on a night that I can still remember, I let it go completely.

I saw that I needed to reject all belief systems, even one as infinitely malleable as Taoism, because they all did a bad thing to the mind and to the will: they made you weaker by virtue of their ideas. Built into them were unappealing social norms and equally unappealing ideas about abiding by — and being controlled by — unseen universal laws. "The Way" struck me as just as dangerous as "God," just as much a superstition, just as much a crutch to avoid accepting the human condition. In one long breath I let all that fear and superstition go.

Is it okay that life is "just" secular, natural, and atheistic? It is. I can find "my way" without bothering myself about "the Way," I can be present without elevating presence into a dogma, I can enjoy the things of this world — like my business and my family — without treating them as mere illusions or poor facsimiles of some invisible perfect flow. And I can use my mind to better purposes than trying to reconcile disagreements among Taoist scholars! The mind is a terrible thing to waste on superstitions, and I am thrilled to have my mind return from its indulgent philosophical wanderings.

REBECCA'S STORY

I grew up on the West Side of Manhattan in a fairly observant Jewish household. We kept kosher, we attended services for the high holidays, and we hosted the celebrations for holidays like Passover for the extended family. I especially loved the celebrations where I could be very grown-up and theatrical and read my Torah pieces like a little Sarah Bernhardt. The more we honored the suffering of the Jews, the more I felt special, not persecuted, and the more swelled my head got, especially because it looked like every great intellectual achievement could be traced to a Jew — whether it was a Freud, a Marx, or an Einstein.

The only problem was, God made no sense to me. So for the longest time I thought of myself as a "cultural Jew" who was somehow holding God as some kind of metaphor for something I could believe in, like nature or maybe spirit. After college, I joined a very liberal congregation with a female rabbi, and most of what we talked about were social issues like peace and justice. We didn't make a very big deal about God, and you could easily have been an atheist and a member of our congregation, so little did God factor into our daily affairs. The camaraderie and the potlucks were great, and we spoke a common language — and yet I couldn't really get over the fact that everything we did was at least nominally based on a God idea that I found preposterous.

The rupture came when some folks joined our congregation who wanted to make a bigger thing out of God. They wanted us to actually believe! — which isn't so preposterous an idea, if you are claiming to be a religious Jew. How can you take offense if someone comes to your church wanting to actually believe in God? I saw that I was the one with the problem, not them. As long as I kept up my lukewarm attachment to Judaism as a religion I was placing myself in an untenable position. I didn't want to be a happy hypocrite who stayed with her congregation because the potluck evenings were so convivial. So I left the congregation — and my religion — for good.

Now I do all the same social and political activities that I did when I belonged to the congregation, only now I do them as a secular humanist. I retained a few of my old friends, those who never cared about God one way or the other, I have new activist friends, and I feel that a weight has been lifted from my shoulders, a weight that I didn't understand had been burdening me so much. I thought that there was no cost to paying lip service to belief, but in fact there had been a huge cost. I had been less honest with my children, less honest with my husband, and less honest with myself all the while I was paying that lip service. Now I am much more able to tell the truth in everything I do — which is an enormous bonus.

You may find yourself not actually believing in gods and not agreeing with the tenets of your religion. If you find yourself in that position, consider the possibility that you have been strongly affected by your religious environment, and that, if only you could get free of those inculcated thoughts, you would be an atheist. You may discover that you are much closer than you think to shedding your disempowering and dangerous beliefs in gods and freeing yourself to live more happily and more powerfully. Millions who formerly believed have freed themselves — and you can too.

CHAPTER THREE

We Make
Our Own Meaning

(What a Remarkable Idea!)

We are quintessentially natural beings. But how should we define ourselves? We'd better not even try! The moment you put a modifier in front of *human being*, you have gone a long way toward distorting human reality. To say that a human being is a learner, a killer, self-interested, generous, social, a loner, a toolmaker, sentient, part-lizard, part-leopard, an explorer, a savage, compassionate — the list of possible attributes is endless — is to distort reality. Human beings are human beings, possessed of everything that connotes and entails.

Once we announce that human beings are everything that human beings are — everything! — then we can decide where we want to focus our energies and attention. On your atheist's way, you may want to focus on your human aptitude for pleasure, on your human aptitude for service, on your human aptitude for love, on your human aptitude for creativity, on your human aptitude for sacrifice, on your human aptitude for leading — all the while remembering that the thing you have chosen is just one of the ways available to you and just one of your endowments. It is vital to remember that each way is just one way: to call this or that *the* way is to conveniently forget how many righteous, fascinating paths are available to us and how often we may find it necessary to change our path because of shifting circumstances.

Of the many ways available to us, I think that one in particular is especially rich. Therefore, I will spend many chapters describing it. It is the way of the passionate meaning-maker, the way of a person who says the following to herself: "Meaning, value, and purpose are human ideas. I will make sense of them for myself and embrace the conclusions that I reach with great passion. As constrained as I am by the facts of existence, I will nevertheless lead with my freedom, acting less instinctually and defensively than I might otherwise act and carefully formulating how I will marry my desires with my sense of duty. Whether it is a decision about the next hour or the next year, a decision about a simple task or the choosing of a career, a decision about a stranger or my mate of thirty years, I will do a special thing that is part of my human repertoire: I will do the thing that will make me proud, the thing most in keeping with what I want my life to signify."

This way allows a person to act in accordance with what I believe are signature truths about reality: 1) that human meaning is subjective and malleable; 2) that self-interest can be discussed internally, leading to thoughtful decisions about what we intend our life to signify; and 3) that because this process is available to us, we can create ourselves in our own best image, marrying "high values" and ordinary pleasures in such a way that we feel proud about ourselves, while getting a full measure of happiness out of life.

This idea of making meaning is at the center of the atheist's way that I'm proposing. As I write this I am sitting at a desk in a Greenwich Village apartment, looking out an east-facing window at a sweltering, smoggy Manhattan summer afternoon. Many of the millions of people who come into Manhattan each day to work are simply trying to cope. Several million folks who reside here live in intense, debilitating poverty. Millions more are working at decent-enough jobs that serve to pay the staggering rents here but that do nothing to serve the intellectual or existential needs of these hard workers. A significant number are wealthy and nevertheless must send their children to psychiatrists in order to deal with irritable bowel syndrome, chronic fatigue, anxiety, apathy, or one of the other difficulties of privilege. Countless numbers are taking the most often prescribed medication in America, antidepressants.

Having received zero training in meaning-making, having never heard the term, having no idea that meaning is the problem and also the answer, this metropolitan multitude, and billions of people worldwide, move from commute to drudgery to commute to dinner and a few drinks, relentlessly shut down, not because they don't have a brain, a heart, and other life-saving equipment but because they are completely unschooled in the ways of meaning. They are alive, but they are not engaged in the project of their own lives.

No one has taught them otherwise. Why aren't we offered any existential training? Because one of society's unacknowledged goals is to minimize existential thought. A company making widgets doesn't want you to wonder about the meaningfulness of its widget. It wants you to be attracted by the widget's design and to buy two of them. A Broadway producer wants you to tap your feet; a police officer wants you to obey; a politician wants you to vote for her; a clergyman wants you to opt for his religion. None of them are likely to invite you to step back and ponder the meaning of their product, policy, or ideology. You are supposed to buy, to agree, and not to think hard about anything. That is what society wants and believes it needs from you.

The very design of our schools — of all schools, since schools are always conservative in intent — supports this antiexistential agenda. You do not get subjects like "thinking for yourself" or "identifying meaningful life projects" in school. You get arithmetic, history, and French. You do not get justice as a subject; you get economics. You do not get rebellion as a subject; you get civics. You may be taught how to do physics but not whether doing physics is of any value. It is made to seem completely self-evident: we teach biology, chemistry, and English here — and the exam will be on Thursday. Oh, and you can take Beginning Mandarin if you like, and Digital Photography. But nothing subversive or existential!

Most parents are no braver than most teachers, principals, or superintendents. They demand that no one in the family discuss meaning, since such discussions would as a matter of course challenge adult authority. What parents allow their children to challenge the family's religious beliefs, drinking habits, or mealtime customs? And so Lutheran parents produce Lutheran children, Catholic parents produce Catholic children, Baptist parents produce Baptist children, simply by not allowing them to be otherwise, and no one finds this telling or objectionable. The child does arithmetic and history by day and sports in the afternoon;

he entertains himself in the evening, and does Lutheran things on Sunday. Nowhere on this schedule do we find penciled in any engagement with or contemplation of meaning.

The net result of this unconscious conspiracy never to discuss meaning is that people learn to hold vapid conversations with themselves and with those around them, conversations meant to keep meaning issues at bay. Then they wonder why they feel listless, empty-headed, and unfulfilled. As a further consequence they begin to fail themselves, since they are rudderless and do not know what to value or where to devote their energy. They also begin to cultivate an unhealthy narcissism, one that accompanies a lack of self-examination and an absence of existential reasoning. By not examining their existential situation, many become full of themselves and manifest a telling grandiosity.

When someone notices all this — and you certainly have noticed it, or you wouldn't have been attracted to this book — a common reaction is disbelief mixed with loathing and incipient depression. You see this culture-wide lack of existential feeling, a lack supported and promoted by every cultural institution, from the bank on the corner to the ward politician, and you are provoked to do more than shake your head: you are provoked to doubt the meaningfulness of anything. In a world where meaning is never discussed and where even occasional conversations about meaning never break out, an existentially sensitive individual is inclined to secretly throw in the towel, even as she goes about the business of her life.

This is the common situation. You know that you have existential needs. You know that the culture does not honor such needs and that in its everyday practices it is opposed to existential examination. At the same time you recognize that some people share your existential intelligence and your existential concerns. You would love to better understand how to lead a life as meaningful as possible and to identify those values really worth "getting behind." You are open to looking at the intricacies of meaning: actually, nothing interests you more. What ought you to do? Let's take a look.

FORTHRIGHTLY ADDRESSING
YOUR MEANING ISSUES

You must take the bull by the horns and become a meaning expert, someone who understands better than the next person that your life is an ever-changing project that requires your constant analysis, your participation, your wits, and your courage. It requires your constant analysis because *all meaning is subjective*: the only way you can opt for settled meaning, objective meaning, or received meaning is by giving away your freedom. You could end your meaning challenges with a full-on lobotomy or by allowing others to tell you what to value, but these are not very attractive options. Your better option is to forthrightly decide what you will reckon as meaningful as you monitor your meaning needs and accept that your meanings are bound to shift and change.

Consider the following example. On Monday, you pledge to yourself to get fit and to take care of your body. On Tuesday, getting some devastating news about your son's health, you offer up one of your organs to save his life, putting your own body at risk. On Wednesday (some months later, having recovered from your operation), hearing troubling news about a threat to your country, you support your son's decision to enlist, even though enlisting constitutes a threat to his life, the life you just gave one of your organs to save. On Thursday (of the following month), having learned more about the war in question, you protest your country's involvement and you wish that your child could come back from that war — right now.

Each action you took came from a different meaning orientation. Each new meaning orientation superseded and even flat-out contradicted a previous one. First, preserving your body was among your very highest concerns. Then, in the blink of an eye, it slipped to a place below a new value and a new meaning, that of saving your son's life. Yet very soon thereafter you accepted the proposition that, however valuable his life might be, he was still acting correctly in putting his life in jeopardy in defense of his country. But the shifting didn't stop there. A month later that proposition no longer felt true, not with the war now seeming wrongheaded and corrupt. What happened? You didn't merely "change your mind" each time. You didn't just hold a new opinion. By thinking through what you wanted to value *right now*, you experienced earthquake-size shifts of meaning.

Meaning — what we value, how we construe our life's purpose, what we make of the facts of existence — is a supremely subjective affair. Two people may agree; a billion people may agree; but they are doing so because they have arrived at the same subjective place, just as a billion others may disagree with them, because they construe their meaning differently. To take one example, it is neither objectively meaningful to explore space or objectively meaningful not to explore space. You can make arguments on either side having to do with humankind's innate need to explore, the advantages to a nation that can wage war from outer space, the squandering of resources better spent on feeding and housing the poor, and so on. You can — and no doubt do —

have an opinion about space exploration, that is, a subjective sense of the meaningfulness or meaninglessness of space exploration. But that is all there is: there is absolutely no objective truth about whether space exploration is or isn't meaningful *since there is no one in charge of meaning except individuals*. You experience something as meaningful, or you don't — who cares if the meaning police assert that you ought to have found it meaningful? Whatever they are saying is just *their* subjective, self-interested opinion.

If further proof were needed of the nonexistence of gods in addition to the proofs usually offered, this truth about subjective meaning would be a kind of ultimate proof. No rational person supposes that gods make us believe in a given war one minute and make us doubt it the next or make us believe that painting is a meaningful way to spend our time and then make us change our mind and decide that taking photographs is more meaningful. If you currently believe in gods, do you really think that gods are shifting those meanings on you? No: that shifting is completely a function of the way that competing interests within you combine with your new experiences. Your new internal arguments and changing real-world events produce in you nothing less than a new view of the world: a new view of *your* world.

Meaning is private, personal, individual, and subjective. Every argument for the objectivity of meaning is merely someone's attempt to elevate her subjective experience and her opinions above yours and mine. Whether or not we move ahead with space exploration has nothing whatsoever to do with the innate meaningfulness of the endeavor — there being none — and everything to do with who gets to decide. Whether you find it more meaningful to sit for an hour by a pond watching ducks paddle or more meaningful to hop up after two minutes and rush home to work on your screenplay is entirely your decision — and one that you might change tomorrow. Who else but you could decide how you intend to order your values, manifest your ethics, and construe meaning? To honor your freedom, you must evaluate and arbitrate the meaning in your life.

People customarily address these "meaning issues" in one or another of several inferior ways. One way is to shrug their shoulders and try to ignore the problem. This sounds like, "I don't know what 'meaning' means, and I'm not interested." A second is to hunt for meaning as if it were a lost treasure. This sounds like, "I will know what life means once I get to the top of the mountain." A third is to bow to the authority of others, abdicating personal responsibility. This sounds like, "I do what God says." A fourth is to take a truth, that there is only subjective meaning, and run with it in the direction of unbridled self-interest. This sounds like, "Everything is permitted, and I can do whatever I damn well please." A fifth is to stare too long at the reality that we are merely excited matter, here for a little while and at the mercy of the fates, and collapse in existential pain. This sounds like, "Nothing I do really matters, given my puny status in an indifferent universe."

These are the usual ways we deal with our meaning issues. But these ways — shrugging meaning away, hunting for meaning, taking meaning orders, using "the problem of meaning" as a cover for selfishness, and feeling defeated in the face of human reality — are all poor choices. There is a better way, better because it acknowledges your unwillingness to bury your head in the sand; it honors your storehouse of experience, a storehouse that makes seeking unnecessary; it matches your desire for freedom, a desire that renders obedience an obscenity; it aligns with your desire to take ethical action, a desire that makes rationalizing selfishness intolerable; and it agrees with your understanding of the pointlessness of pointlessness — your understanding that nihilism, whatever its attraction, is simply not a sensible option. You reject these five as unworthy, and you choose a sixth option: passionate meaning-making.

You start by realizing that the universe has set you up with a certain peculiar dilemma. It has created a you that can comprehend the absurd challenges that you face, among them having to deal with your mortality and your meaning needs, and then left you marooned and perplexed. It has built you to have a lifelong love affair with truth, beauty, and goodness, then pulled back the curtain to reveal how a lie may serve your ends better than the truth does, that smog produces gorgeous sunsets, and that "goodness" may mean having to destroy your enemy. You discover into what quagmires terms such as *ethical action* and *meaningful work* take you. And you discover, ready or not, that you must trudge neck-deep into that quagmire.

CREATE YOURSELF

When our younger daughter came home from college one year she presented me with a coffee mug. The mug had a motto: "Life isn't about finding yourself. Life is about creating yourself." "Isn't that your philosophy in a nutshell?" she laughed. She was exactly right. E. W. Wilcox, to whom the quote is attributed, had captured the essence of thousands of years of existential thought: that life is as much a responsibility as a gift and that each of us is honor-bound to create ourselves in our own best image.

I make my meaning — or I don't. All that exists until I actively and mindfully make personal meaning is the possibility of meaning and, while I wait to get started, the experience of emptiness. There is the possibility that I will experience the next hour as meaningful, a possibility that turns into a reality only if I make a certain kind of decision and a certain kind of investment. If I don't make that decision and that investment, I feel I am just going through the motions and wasting my precious time. We've all had that experience — many of us far too much of the time.

We are on the threshold of understanding a shining idea: that each individual's life can have meaning, even if the universe has none. Each of us comes with appetites, genetic predispositions, and everything else that *human being* connotes, and still we are free to choose what meaning we intend to make. Nature has granted us this. I get to decide what will make me feel righteous and happy, and you get to decide what will make you feel righteous and happy. You can turn the meaning that was waiting to be made into the meaning of your life.

You and you alone are the sole arbiter of the meaning in your life. The second you turn to someone and say, "What does life mean?" or, "What should my life mean?" you have slipped into a mind-set that courts inauthenticity and depression. The second you agree with someone simply because of her position or reputation, whether that someone is a guru, author, cleric, parent, politician, general, or elder, you fall from the path of personal meaning-maker.

You and you alone get to decide. That is the awesome proposition facing every modern person. The revolutionary idea that I'm proposing is that, as limited as we are in a biological and psychological sense, we are exactly that free in an existential sense. If we do not live that way, honoring that existential freedom, we get sad and depressed. If we do not live that way, we find ourselves wishing that we had opted for authenticity and had decided to matter.

I understand completely the extent to which people are burdened by the feeling that they and their efforts do not matter. It isn't that people don't work hard. They do. But two thoughts, that they are disposable throwaways in a meaningless universe and that nothing they do can possibly alter that painful truth, play havoc beneath the surface, draining them of motivational energy and fitting them for a depression. These doubts must be met in the following way. You announce that meaning does not exist until you make it, and then you don the mantle of meaning-maker. The minute you do this, all previous belief systems, both those that told you what to believe and those that told you that there was nothing to believe, vanish. You suddenly enact the paradigm shift that I believe we are now ready to embrace: *the shift from seeking meaning to making meaning.*

You let go of wondering what the universe wants of you, you let go of the fear that nothing matters, and you announce that you will make life mean exactly what you intend it to mean. This is an amazing, glorious, and triumphant announcement. The instant you realize that meaning is not provided (as traditional belief systems teach) and that it is not absent (as nihilists feel), a new world of potential opens up for you. You suddenly have the opportunity to pursue personally resonant activities and the philosophical and psychological pillars to support those pursuits. You break free of tradition, with its restrictions, demands, and narcissistic bent, and set out to make your life a thing of value. You haven't made it that thing yet, simply by announcing your intention, but you have aimed yourself in a brilliant direction: the direction of your own creation.

CHAPTER FOUR

We Invest Meaning

(Another Curious Idea!)

I was chatting about this book with the same daughter who gave me the "Life is about creating yourself" coffee mug. At one point she laughed wryly and said, "Do you ever define *meaning* in the book? I bet you don't!" Of course she was right. I won't and can't define *meaning* here. I could try, but it would amount to many thousands of words making distinctions among ideas like purpose, significance, importance, intention, epic metaphor, enlightened self-interest, and so on. That conversation could be interesting, or it could amount to tiresome hairsplitting. But in either case I intend to skip it.

However, I expect that by the end of our discussion we will have circled the elephant carefully enough that we will have a solid sense of what *meaning* means. We do need that solid sense — and a vocabulary to go with it. For we need to be able to understand and comfortably employ terms like *investing meaning*, *meaning crisis*, *meaning substitute*, *meaning adventure*, and many related ones. This is the language of the atheist's way: our shared vocabulary of meaning. However, we can't get there directly, or all at once.

Not long ago I asked many folks to answer the following three questions: 1) What do you take the term *making meaning* to mean?; 2) What do you take the term *investing meaning* to mean?; and 3) If you've ever consciously made a meaning investment, how was that experience different from an ordinary experience? My correspondents had no problem understanding these three questions, and I suspect that you don't either. They did not need any terms defined or any long explanations. They understood perfectly well that I was asking them about how they value life, how they conceptualize their life purpose, and how they differentiate "ordinary time" from "time better spent." Here is a sampling of their answers to the third question, "If you've ever consciously made a meaning investment, how was that experience different from an ordinary experience?"

Max, a financial analyst and actor, wrote:

> About eight years ago, when I'd gotten tired of looking for employment in the financial services industry, I started playing around with the idea of doing other things. I had always been curious about acting. Breathing deeply, and telling myself that I could do this, that I could honor a promise to myself to participate wholeheartedly in a personal experiment, I was able to open the front door of an acting studio and attend the first day of an acting class.
>
> I went through all the exercises that day and on subsequent days. Many of them felt absolutely stupid. But eventually I began to have fun. For our final project, we each had to

deliver a monologue in front of the class — horror of horrors. So I memorized mine until I was mumbling it in my sleep. My presentation was terrible. I was completely defensive. My character was angry, so I strutted about and ranted and shouted my lines. My classmates were quiet. I think maybe they were just politely suppressing their laughter — or maybe just looking on in horror that they would appear equally foolish when their turn came.

The instructor calmed me down. I had really embarrassed myself, but I promised myself that I would stay, no matter what, so I complied with his instructions. I started again, began my monologue quietly, and allowed the emotion to build slowly and naturally. He continued directing me, and I could feel the shift. Something strange started to happen. I noticed that the director was no longer speaking. I noticed that people in the audience were getting emotional in various ways, and that these emotions were growing. I got this strange sense of strength that I had never known before. Somehow, I don't know how, I knew to say the last few words of the monologue in almost a whisper. As I finished, I looked squarely at the group, quietly got up out of my chair, and gave one of those "ah, forget it!" gestures and walked offstage.

The instructor congratulated me and told me that my performance was the best he had ever heard with that monologue. To this day, that is one of my proudest achievements. And also to this day, if I get a bit nervous before I act I just take a deep breath and remember that moment, start quietly, and allow the strength to build. I knew that I had "invested meaning" in that class and refused to just walk away from it; and, although I was scared and embarrassed, I also made a meaning investment in that moment onstage, an investment that allowed me to take direction, feel and use my own power, and

become something that I never dreamed I could become — a
real actor.

Pamela, a painter, recalled:

A few weeks ago I visited some Chelsea art galleries in won-
derful autumn weather. After a while my good mood left me.
The artwork that I saw that day was not at all inspiring to me.
I thought to myself, This is my goal? Suddenly the idea of
exhibiting in these galleries seemed meaningless. Therefore
making art seemed meaningless also. I had made a big effort
to arrange my life so that I had time to focus on art, and now
it didn't seem important.

When I got back to my studio it was really hard to paint.
Then I realized that I had a choice, to continue feeling bad or
to think of a way for my art to have meaning to me so that I'd
feel motivated to do it. I decided that my art would be a positive force and uplifting to people — I "invested meaning" in
that idea — and just like that, my motivation to paint returned.
I decided that making my art was meaningful in part because
it had the potential to be meaningful to others.

From that moment on I've painted steadily. I've also been
back to those Chelsea galleries — and I've enjoyed being
there, not so much because of the art on the walls but because
other people are there on any given sunny Saturday afternoon
enjoying themselves and benefiting from the experience. Yes,
many art pieces are not to my liking and in my estimation are
revered for the wrong reasons. But that isn't to say that art
doesn't serve. I am "invested" in the idea that art can serve, and
I again find it meaningful to paint. I appreciate that I might
change my mind once again — that meaning is that kind of
thing — but at least for several weeks now meaning has felt
rock-steady.

Andrew, a police officer, told the following story:

I had always wanted to be a police officer and never had any problems with meaning. For me, being a police officer, a member of my community, and a family man provided a full meaning plate. The reality of being on the force was everything that I hoped it would be, and I found every day exciting, energizing, exacting, and exactly how I wanted to spend my time on earth. I was right where I wanted to be.

The problems began when I got partnered with a corrupt cop, a man who was fifteen years my senior and a bully and a crook. I understand the realities of policing and I know that sometimes you can't go by the book, but my partner was going way beyond mere shortcuts — he was doing tremendous harm and betraying our sacred trust. At the same time, I know how murderous to a career it can be to turn in a fellow cop. For months I stewed about what to do — no decision has ever been harder, because I hated the idea of jeopardizing my job, especially over such a creep.

Finally I realized that my values wouldn't allow me to do nothing or to foist my partner onto somebody else. It makes perfect sense to call what I did next making a conscious meaning investment, because meaning had previously come easily to me; this time the situation was different. This time I had to do something really difficult in order to align my life with my values. To make the rest of the story short, I turned my partner in and lived to tell the tale — and to continue on the job. Will there be some repercussions to my career? Maybe yes, maybe no. But I know that it was the absolutely right meaning investment to make.

Sara, a teacher, recalled:

I've had a long history of depression — and of confronting depression. Depression was always the enemy, or the fatal flaw, and I spent much of my life feeling defeated, deflated, and powerless, even though I had some decent accomplishments in life as a teacher and a mentor of teachers. One day I decided to rewrite my depression as a hero's journey — and that changed everything. My depression became my "worthy enemy," and struggling with it taught me to understand the value of my passion and my life — and the value of myself. I think that I made a meaning investment in life, if that's the way to put it.

From that point on I could relate to others fighting this enemy and, through my teaching and in other ways, offer some insight and healing. I stalked depression and learned about that core in me that is untouched by depression. I began to touch the distant shores of joy, claim that land, put some of its sand in my pocket, and take it home with me. From this journey, part of me has been transformed, and I have moved at least part of the way from victimhood and woundedness to vital aliveness. What did I make the meaning investment in? I'm not sure I can quite say: maybe in my chance to have a good life. But I know that I made such an investment on the day that I decided to rewrite my life as a hero's journey.

Marcia, a writer, photographer, and activist, answered this way:

In addition to being an essayist and photographer, I'm an environmental activist. While serving as environmental commission chair for my local community, I was hit with trumped-up charges by a township committeeman who wanted me removed from office. This was a surprise ploy, done at a public meeting, in front of many people. Since I was a volunteer, it would have been less stressful for me to just walk away. I could have legitimately said, "Who needs this aggravation?" But I made a conscious decision to fight and use the incident to shine a bright light into the darkest corners of our local government.

Months of severe stress followed, until the committee backed off in the face of overwhelming and sustained public opposition. The incident was seen as so egregious an abuse of power that it was instrumental in helping vote the incumbents out of office. The personal meaning I had invested struck a chord of meaning in others. Since I strive very hard to do things that have meaning (to me), I'm not sure that this event really differed from my ordinary experience, except perhaps in depth or degree. But having to draw a line in the sand and say, "This far and no farther" cut to the core of my being much more than most things I do. So in one sense it was not an unusual meaning investment, since I make them all the time, but in another sense it was, because it was more dramatic, more difficult, more stressful — and maybe worthier.

Carlos, a pilot, said:

I'd always wanted to fly, and I went the incredibly arduous route of getting into the Air Force Academy and becoming an air force pilot. I'd dreamed of flying jets, but through a mixture of circumstances and bad luck I ended up flying transports. That held much less meaning for me than flying fighters, and I began to resent being just a glorified bus driver. I had a lot of years to put in, and I tried to make the best of my ongoing meaning crisis, but I started getting very down on myself (and on the air force) and began to fantasize about getting out and never flying again.

After twelve years in the service, there came a point when I could go for retirement. I had so much invested in the military, and the retirement package was so attractive, that it made no logical sense to give up all those benefits. But existentially I saw that I had to make a change. I made what I would now call a conscious meaning investment in researching my flying options after the military. I didn't want to work for a big airline and continue my "glorified bus driving," so I asked myself the question, "What kind of flying would really serve my meaning needs?" One day, surfing the Net, I found what I was looking for: a company that specialized in flying doctors into remote South American locations. That was it! I knew that doing that kind of flying would perfectly combine my values, my desires, and my dreams.

As it happened, I could speak and write both Spanish and Portuguese. I contacted the company and, to make a long story short, I now fly into Amazon jungle locations bringing in vital medical care. Every time I enter the cockpit of my small plane I feel like I am investing meaning in something rich, valuable, and beyond reproach. I also married a Brazilian woman, and we have a small son. This blessing feels like it directly flowed out of making a mindful choice to be of service, forsaking the amazing (but only financial) benefits that staying in the air force would have provided, and finding a way to marry my love of flying with my value system.

Let me recap for a moment and put these responses in context. There are no gods. The universe takes no particular interest in you and me. We live, we die, and while we are here we are exactly what we are: human beings, members of a particular species, and certain kinds of creatures. To define what we are is to reduce and distort what we are: to say that we are nothing but our desires or nothing but our self-interest is to misrepresent us.

We do not say that the rose is its fragrance. It is everything that constitutes "rose." We do not say that the bee is its buzz. It is everything that constitutes "bee." We, in turn, are everything human: indifferent, curious, selfish, caring, excited, bored, friendly, unfriendly, interested in our own lives, disinterested in our own lives, arrogant, frightened, sober, addicted, and so on.

From this exact and vast endowment we get to choose how we intend to live, since choosing is also part of our endowment. This choosing I am calling "making meaning"; the action that goes with this choosing I am calling "investing meaning."

Investing meaning and related terms such as *reinvesting meaning* and *withdrawing meaning* do a nice job of capturing the flavor of what making meaning entails. We look forthrightly at the next hour, the next week, the next month, the next year, and even the next decade, and we try to make conscious decisions about what we intend to value, how we intend to spend our time, and what actions are congruent with our heroic effort to live passionately and well. We will need to say more about where to make these meaning investments, how to balance our immediate meaning needs with our long-term meaning needs, and so on, but we have made a start. Our next step is an examination of the process whereby you nominate yourself a passionate meaning-maker and the hero of your own story.

CHAPTER FIVE

We Nominate Ourselves

(As the Heroes of Our Own Stories)

Before you can make meaning, an odd kind of election process must occur. You must nominate yourself as the meaning-maker in your life and as the hero of your own story. Then you must consciously elect yourself to that position. You must decide to put yourself before everything and everyone else, not in a grandiose, egotistical, or narcissistic way but in a way that reflects the idea that you alone decide what meaning you intend to make. By affirming that you intend to fill your days with meaning and by making meaning investments in accordance with an enlightened understanding of self-interest, you meet your existential obligations to yourself, you make yourself proud, and you rise to the occasion.

You nominate yourself to be the one who will courageously do what you think ought to be done, even if everyone is pressing you to do something else. You nominate yourself to be the one who will decide if manipulating paint on canvas or advocating for a particular cause is or isn't a meaningful activity: you will not let your mother, your lover, your god, your mayor, your neighbor, your teacher, or your boss decide. You nominate yourself to decide every meaning-related and ethics-related issue in your life.

Few people actually nominate themselves in this way. Most defer to the meaning-making apparatus of their culture, taking comfort in the fact that others have built a meaning nest for them. This built-in cover allows them to avoid taking responsibility and at the same time causes them to grow grandiose, narcissistic, and egotistical. As soon as you put on the robes of your culture and add gravity to your mere humanness by wearing the badge of your profession, your club, your gang, or your clan, you participate in life more selfishly. The judge who is a political hack, the professor who has built her reputation on a theory that she refuses to examine, the cleric who sees his job as filling the seats on the high holidays — these are some examples of people who refuse to engage in the process of personal meaning-making, with its requirements of honesty and self-awareness.

To nominate yourself as the hero of your own story is to step outside society, not with the intention of turning your back on it but with the intention of not allowing it to dictate to you. In literature and in mythology, a character who nominates himself in this way begins an epic and heroic journey: epic and heroic in large part because he sets himself up from the outset as an individual who will not be dictated to by cultural pressure. He is the lone gunslinger who does not belong to either side in the dispute between the cattle ranchers and the sheep ranchers. This hero looks at his culture, sees its hypocrites and its dupes, and announces, "I will go my own way." In books and movies, this individual is regularly nominated not only by himself but by others as well: by the ordinary townsfolk who beg him to save their town, their world, or their galaxy because they see that he has the strength and integrity that they lack.

He may agree to save their town, as the hero does in *High Noon*, or he may stroll right out of town, as Clint Eastwood's character often does, but whether he decides to help or to leave, he remains singular and separate, an honest witness to what is happening. In this regard he is always a leader, because he will not follow. It is impossible to nominate yourself as the meaning-maker in your own life and also to follow. You may join, you may serve, you may put someone else's interests before your own, but none of that is the same as following. "I nominate myself" means "I won't follow." This isn't hubris: it is simply the fruit of your decision to live on your own terms.

When I nominate myself and begin to make my meaning, I can't then quote Scripture, the law, an opinion poll, expert evidence, tradition, or anything else as the reason for my life decisions. What I must say is, "I've thought it over and decided." If you badger me about why I have made the decision I have made — whether to write a certain sort of novel, go out on strike, marry someone of a different race, or drop everything and mount a protest — I can only repeat myself: "I've thought it over and decided." I have actually done more than merely thought it over — that is too simple a way of saying how meaning gets made — but it is a decent shorthand answer. I am happy to add, "It might be a mistake; who knows." I am happy to listen to the opinions of others (if I am in that sort of mood). But I know that the decision is mine to make. I have nominated myself, elected myself, and that's where the buck stops: with me.

The following is a report from Barbara, who nominated herself in just this fashion:

When I thought of nominating myself, I was reminded of the first line of *David Copperfield*: "Whether I shall turn out to be the hero of my own life, or whether that station will be held by anybody else, these pages must show." Growing up, I knew without question that I did not share my family's values or those of any of the people I lived among. On the one hand, I was bold enough to choose to go my own way. On the other, I was unwise enough to expect that I would find the validation of "my way" out in the world. That put me in the position of believing that I needed to find public support for my visual art right away, before I'd actually acquired sufficient skills in either craft or personal strength.

I stubbornly refused any support that came my way, believing that to take such support was to cave in. I had misunderstood what it meant to nominate myself: I got the part about living by my own values right, but I added on an unnecessary part about never listening to others or accepting help. After some years of blight, it came as both a shock and a blessing to finally realize that it was not only my right to nominate myself but also a certain kind of responsibility, one that included a mature appraisal of how to allow the reality and values of others into my life.

As soon as I accepted this fuller sense of self-nomination, I freed myself to balance the idea that I was the only real source of self-validation with the idea that others could be allowed to count in more than nominal ways. As a result I've made progress in winning support from mentors and from unveiling my work to various publics, including the commercial marketplace. Of course, I have to be careful: I have to be wary of the many forces — family, friends, colleagues, bosses, and the repetitive power of pop culture — that can influence me if I let them. To nominate myself as the hero of my own life means permitting others into my life, but it also means staying awake to the main idea that I must decide on my course of action.

You may prefer a different phrase to stand for this self-nomination process. Some people like "I select myself." Others like "I choose myself." You are the final arbiter. But many people like the phrase "I nominate myself."

Louise, for instance, explained why she does:

"I nominate myself" is definitely the best way of saying it for me, maybe because I've been so involved in local politics this year, but I think it goes beyond that. The phrase evoked a picture of me striding ahead through a stiff wind, and that is pretty much how my life normally is. "I nominate myself" just resonates for me, as does the reluctant hero analogy and the idea that I can't be a follower. I see myself rather like the lead sled dog — I feel as if I instinctively know the way, and I don't want to waste precious time wandering around getting lost or looking at the butts of the dogs in front of me. I want to see the whole, unspoiled big picture — that's what feels true for me.

The Japanese say, "If a nail sticks up, hammer it down." I think our culture says the same thing. There is a price to pay for taking charge of your life, and many people don't want to pay that price. But the reward is as complete a measure of freedom as is possible for human beings, living a life of integrity and self-actualization. So I accept the consequences of the nomination process and elect myself as the hero of my own story.

DONNING THE MANTLE OF MEANING-MAKER

It isn't at all easy to say, "I am a meaning-maker." First, it sounds a little pompous and arrogant. Who am I to make meaning? How self-important that sounds! Second, it flies in the face of tradition. Most traditions ask you to blend in, to serve, and to bow to the common will. Third, it isn't transparently clear what the phrase means or what you might be agreeing to. For these and other reasons, you may stop on the threshold of announcing that you are a meaning-maker and take an involuntary step backward. Though the mantle of meaning-maker is there for you to don, you shake your head and refuse. Let me try to meet your objections one by one.

The first objection is that donning the mantle of meaning-maker is an arrogant, pompous, self-important thing to do. At the heart of this objection is a misunderstanding of the difference between standing up for your cherished beliefs and principles, which you know is not an arrogant thing to do, and squashing other people underfoot, a position you are right to condemn. "I am living by my principles" is not identical to "You do not count." Does it feel arrogant to say, "I am living by my principles?" No; I think it feels exactly the opposite. I think it feels grounded, humble, sincere, and honorable.

Still, it may *feel* arrogant. We have so many injunctions against saying "This is what I believe, and I wish you wouldn't bully me with your beliefs" that, instead of speaking and acting bravely from a place of personal conviction, we retreat to a familiar place of common agreement. Becoming accustomed to that place and feeling safe there, taking even a small step into the territory of personal belief can feel arrogant and scary. We laugh with the other sophisticated parents about our children's drinking, and only after three of them are killed in a car accident do we say what we believed all along, that there was too much drinking going on. Yesterday it felt too difficult to tell the truth, and today it is easy to tell it, because now everyone is telling it. It would have been much better to tell it yesterday.

A second objection is that to self-nominate and don the mantle of meaning-maker is to break with tradition. Most traditions point a finger at anyone who announces that she knows what she knows and believes what she believes. Indeed, you must break with any tradition that demands any sort of obedience from you. Even in a tradition like Zen Buddhism, in which a central tenet is that no one should claim more knowledge than anyone else, the very hierarchy that produces Zen masters supports the unspoken principle that some people are on top and others should defer to them. So you will need to choose what part of your tradition you can accept — if any. This is most true if you are still a believer in gods and supernatural authority.

Many people do not like to fly in the face of tradition — the very idea makes them feel a little queasy. Tradition is what they know, and it may feel like the glue holding a fragile world together. They say to themselves, "Yes, it is just a tradition, but it serves some purpose, so although I don't really believe in it, I can live with it." Since donning the mantle of meaning-maker involves choosing where to invest and where to divest meaning, a position that forces you to look at your group's traditions with a critical eye, you may step back from making meaning, reluctant and even frightened to examine your traditions.

But the smarter, braver part of you knows that a tradition is only of value if it is of value. It may be your group's tradition to abort girl fetuses, burn witches at the stake, or damn to hell everyone but members of your group. Even the most innocent-seeming family, community, or religious tradition exists solely because of the ability of some authority (like a parent, a ruler, or a cleric) to make demands. As an honest person, you know how unrighteous a reason to honor a tradition that is. Part of you feels that there is something deeply right about tradition, and part of you knows that a given tradition ought to be honored only if it is honorable and worthy. Be brave and look at your traditions with open eyes. Start by reminding yourself that the mere existence of a tradition is not a good reason to honor it — and surely not a good reason to avoid nominating yourself as the hero of your own story.

A third objection is that *making meaning* is an obscure and even unintelligible term. It is easy to throw up your hands and cry, "I don't get the idea of meaning-making. How can you *make* meaning? Either there is meaning or there isn't. You can't just make meaning like you can make a car or a violin. No, I don't get it — so I think I'll pass!" This objection is at once reasonable and disingenuous. It is disingenuous because billions of people easily buy concepts like Holy Spirit, karma, or nirvana without blinking an eye. Is making meaning harder to understand than "nirvana"? In fact, making meaning is a crystal-clear idea. We know perfectly well that it consists of ideas such as personal responsibility, courage, engagement, and authenticity. It is a far *less* mysterious term than the ones that billions of people already employ as pillars of their belief system.

However, part of this objection is not at all disingenuous. It is the part of us that cries out in pain. What we are objecting to is not the obscurity of the term but the nature of the universe that the term posits. We object to a universe in which meaning has to be made. We object to a universe that is meaningless until we force it to mean. We object to nature pulling this dirty trick on us and making us a partner to it, giving us exactly two choices: either not to look this reality square in the eye and live as a coward or to see what is required and live as an absurd hero. It is not the obscurity of the term *making meaning* that disturbs us, but what it says about life.

It is hard to meet the objection that we would like life to be something other than what it is. The only real way to meet this objection is with a certain maturity, by quietly demanding of ourselves that we face the central reality that meaning must be made; and by facing all the peripheral realities as well, for instance, that meaning can be lost in the blink of an eye, that meanings change, and so on. We understand what this maturity feels like, we understand that it is available to us, and we know that when we come from that place we make ourselves proud. All we need to do is stand up straight — which is exactly what you would love to do, isn't it?

A fourth objection is that making meaning demands too much honesty and personal responsibility. How can you smoke two packs of cigarettes a day and also claim to be making meaning? How can you yell at your dog, treating it as a stand-in for your boss, and also claim to be making meaning? How can you watch television four hours every night when your pet project remains untouched and also claim to be making meaning? You can't — and you know it. As long as you prefer not to take responsibility for your life, you will sprint rather than stroll away from the idea of making meaning. And who isn't inclined to avoid all that responsibility?

To protect themselves from too much awareness and to help

them abdicate personal responsibility, many people create a worldview in which responsibility is minimized. They cast blame, announce that everything happens for a reason, invoke fate, consult their chart, or submit to god's will. In a host of ways they protect and defend their desire not to take responsibility for their thoughts, feelings, and behaviors. This is natural — but it does not make them feel proud. The fact that they know better (sometimes only in a remote corner of their consciousness) and the fact that they can be better (as evidenced by the number of people with an addiction who embrace recovery) are the exact answers to this objection.

People would love to take that responsibility and make themselves proud, but they know themselves too well and fear that they are unequal to the task. They have drifted off too many diets, squandered too many hours, and failed to rise to the occasion more times than they care to remember. If this is your history, you can leave it at that, remain disappointed in your efforts, and throw in the towel. Or you can take a deep breath, locate that place inside you that relishes effort and that takes pride in trying, and cast aside this objection. You can say, "All right, I accept full responsibility," since that is exactly what you've always intended to do.

A fifth objection, a cousin to the previous one, is that making meaning is just too much work. You want to kick back — you don't want to make meaning. You want to get the items on your to-do list checked off and be done with work. You don't want to make meaning after seven in the evening, on weekends, on holidays, and around the clock. You want the company picnic, the Saturday movie, the visit with friends, the various ordinary things that you do to be just what they are, simple and ordinary, without adding on this taxing business of judging whether or not they are meaningful. You don't want every passing second to come with this added demand, that you invest it with some meaning. Yikes! It's exhausting just to think about. Fair enough. But our lives are the sorts of epic projects that require work and attention. It is a central tenet of any authentic person's life plan to work at the project of her life, since that work is life: it is the way we justify ourselves, create ourselves, and make ourselves proud. It is the way we love our lives and love life itself.

You accept that making meaning is work, but you construe that work as the loving work of self-creation. It isn't slave labor but the choice you make about how you intend to live. Even if it were slave labor, you might still be able to manage a stoic smile and accept your lot. That is the message in Albert Camus's famous essay "The Myth of Sisyphus," in which the narrator discovers that he can retain his freedom of attitude even though he is sentenced to an eternity of pushing boulders up a mountain. But our meaning-making work isn't slave labor: it is a manifestation of the loving attitude we choose to adopt toward ourselves. Nor do we have to engage in it *all* the time — but that is an idea for a later chapter.

A sixth objection is that making meaning involves too much choosing, which in turn provokes too much anxiety. In fact, choosing does produce anxiety; and constant choosing can indeed produce constant anxiety. We can — and often do — become anxious trying to choose which car to buy, what direction to go in with our careers, or even whether to choose the cereal that tastes good or the cereal that is good for us. To hurry along the choosing process, so as to get past the anxiety that begins to well up, people often make rash decisions. Indeed, most people will do almost anything rather than think too hard or too long about the choices that confront them.

Given this ubiquitous dynamic, that we hate choosing because of the anxiety it produces, it is natural that we will not want to make meaning, a process that amounts to making one reasoned, careful choice after another. If it is so hard choosing which cereal to buy, how much harder will it be choosing where to invest your meaning minute by minute and day by day? Better to stay with a simple routine, keep your head down, move another day closer to retirement, and not think too much about where you are going. Better to do anything than face climbing a mountain of choosing!

This is entirely understandable. But the more you avoid choosing and the more you impulsively or irrationally make the choices you can't avoid, the less free a life you lead. Freedom equals thoughtful choosing. There is no possibility of personal freedom without a commitment to lifelong choosing. When a value that means something to you is at risk, you must make a conscious choice to defend it — or fail yourself by ducking. When work that means something to you is at stake, you must choose to do it — or fail yourself by plopping down in front of the television set. We are always choosing, since "not doing anything" is also a choice, so why not brave the anxiety that comes with frank, forthright choosing and make yourself proud?

A seventh objection relates to the last one: that making meaning increases our core anxiety. Isn't one of our goals to reduce our experience of anxiety, not increase it? If dark tunnels make us anxious, are we obliged to explore them? Can't we just avoid them? How you answer this question determines how you lead your life. If you decide that reducing your experience of anxiety is a paramount goal and that you intend to avoid anxiety at all costs, then you have made yourself susceptible to all blandishments of ease, from laugh tracks to god-talk.

To live authentically, we must consciously *embrace* anxiety. We must *invite* anxiety. Our nervous system says that this is irrational, but our heart knows that it is exactly right. If we intend to make meaning by writing a great novel, we can't also hope to avoid anxiety. If we intend to hunt down a life-saving herb in a mosquito-infested jungle, we can't also hope to avoid anxiety. If we intend to stand up for a principle that our whole town rejects, we can't also hope to avoid anxiety. To accomplish these meaning-making tasks, we are obliged to say, "Okay, anxiety. *Bring it on!*"

We tend to lose our taste for roller coasters the older we get. At fourteen we can't wait to get on the Wild Monkey or the Ultimate Plunge. At forty, we can wait. Likewise, we lose our taste for anxiety. We mind our grandchildren with an even more watchful eye than we minded our children, we make safer investments, and we take fewer risks and invite fewer heart palpitations. This is the natural way. Still, to live authentically, we must never stop risking anxiety, braving anxiety, embracing anxiety, and inviting anxiety. For a meaning-maker, there is no retirement from anxiety, as much as we might wish for one. Once we accept this proposition, we receive an important side benefit: the less desperately we avoid anxiety, the less frequently we experience it. It was all that worry about anxiety that made us so anxious!

An eighth objection is that opting to make meaning guarantees that meaning will never be settled. We rightly conclude that our meanings are bound to change as we decide to invest meaning here, divest meaning there, and monitor our meaning investments. How unsettling to be for a war one day and against it the next, or against it one day and for it the next, as our subjective sense of the war's value changes. We know in our bones that these are among the worst feelings possible, having our sense of the world turned completely upside down. We don't want this to happen, and so we adopt simple positions, like always being for or against a war our country is waging, so as to "settle meaning down" once and for all and spare ourselves meaning earthquakes.

If you fear, by agreeing to don the mantle of meaning-maker, that meaning will never be settled, you are exactly right. You will indeed be opening yourself up to the occasional painful feeling of uncertainty or foolishness. But what you lose in safety, you gain in righteousness. You can live a settled life, existentially speaking, but only at the cost of your integrity. It is really much better, albeit more dangerous, to accept that meaning will never be settled, that meaning is always at risk, and that meaning is a challenge and not a foregone conclusion. Agreeing to this is agreeing to live with earthquakes. There is no reason why you should do this with a smile and no reason why you should feel sanguine about surviving all that tumult. It is simply the right course, since to settle meaning for all time is to kill it off.

Other objections could also be raised. All can be met, but meeting them might tax your patience. I think you understand the main point: that nominating yourself as the hero of your own story and deciding to lead a life devoted to intentional meaning-making come with profound challenges — but so does any sort of thoughtful life. Will you make some choices and some meaning investments that you later regret? Of course. Will you feel unequal to making meaning on a given day? Of course. Still, opting to live this way, as the creator of your life and the hero of your own story, brings the greatest rewards, among them a sense of dignity, real accomplishments, and joy.

CHAPTER SIX

We Get Blue
Sometimes

(Who Doesn't?)

Before we continue our investigations, we need to stop for a
moment and chat about a particular — some would say,
powerful — "practical objection" to the atheist's way. People
antagonistic to atheism are quick to assert that it is better not to
be an atheist, whether or not there are any gods, because entertaining the idea of a disinterested universe devoid of gods is just
too depressing. To put their objection simply, the atheist's way
is a road to depression.

Why not just believe, they argue, if believing provides more
comfort and hope than not believing? Why paint the bleakest
possible picture of the universe, even if that portrait is accurate,
when, just by using our imaginations, we can picture a universe in
which we get many lives, a nice home after death, and our prayers
answered? Isn't that simply the wiser choice, psychologically

speaking? Don't we have enough to be depressed about without adding the sobering thought that we are merely excited matter passing through an indifferent universe?

Furthermore, isn't taking all that responsibility a depressing way to live? Isn't it much more pleasant to chalk up our weaknesses to sin, close our eyes to the needs of civilization, opt for the biggest house and the most expensive cigar, take what isn't nailed down, and forgive ourselves for our transgressions once a week or once a year in a painless little ceremony? Why not choose pleasure, power, selfishness, winning, and the blandishments of belief? Since every path is merely a choice (here our correspondent winks, because he knows that we are obliged to agree with him), why not choose wine, women, and song, throw in a benevolent god who helps your home team win, and scoot depression right out the door?

There are many rejoinders to this argument, including the accurate one that in this view, many different ideas about depression are being conflated. Mixed together are states like grief, despair, sadness, depression with a small "d," Depression with a big "D," regular blues, occasional blues, and so on. Also mixed together are biological, psychological, social, and existential depressions. But the rejoinder that I want to focus on is the following one: that the main premise is false. It is simply not true that atheists, because of their convictions and their worldview, are as a group more depressed than believers. They are certainly more depressed about *some things*, like the sway that religion holds on too many people and the sad brainwashing of children into supernatural belief. But that they are bluer about some things does not mean that they are bluer overall.

Believers and atheists alike get the blues. Human beings feel blue for a limitless number of reasons. We can feel blue when the sun doesn't shine for too many consecutive days. We can feel blue because our brain's been wired to be blue by adverse childhood experiences. We can feel blue because we wanted something and didn't get it. We can feel blue because love walked out the door. We can feel blue because our job bores us. We can feel blue because we feel tyrannized by the repetitive demands of life. To think that there is a medication or a mantra for all these scenarios is to engage in wishful thinking; and to suppose that atheists have cornered the market of these blue notes is nonsense.

We may feel blue because we see clearly, and what we see saddens us. We see that the amount of intelligence displayed by most people may not be intelligence enough for the challenges faced by our species. We see the shadowy outline of ambiguity everywhere: how one person's profit is another person's loss, how one person's terrorist is another person's freedom fighter. We see how much we fall short in our own efforts and how often we break the promises we make to ourselves. Not only are there no medications or charms to combat these realities, but these realities are as disturbing to thoughtful believers as they are to thoughtful atheists. We hold no monopoly on the blues.

It can sadden us to recognize that what we do does not matter a fig to the universe, that no loving spirit is watching over us or waiting for us, and that every human action is exactly as justified or unjustified as the next, as far as the universe is concerned. Atheists see this and, seeing it, get blue. But believers often see these same things and get blue twice over. They get blue, first of all, because of what they see; they get even bluer because what they see makes them doubt their belief system and wonder if they're deceiving themselves. Given this double whammy,

might not the believer be more prone to depression than the
atheist?

FORMER BELIEVERS REPORT

One place to look for the answer to this question is among atheists who formerly believed, since they have experienced both sides
of the coin. For them, believing was itself a source of depression,
and they find themselves much happier, having shed their belief
in gods.

Mary explained:

> Existential depression is only something that I really suffered
> from as a Christian. The Christian worldview, which is that
> man is so depraved that without the sacrifice of another indi-
> vidual he will be tortured for eternity, was always unfath-
> omable and deeply depressing. I found all the following notions
> depressing: that through an accident of birth someone grew up
> to be either evil or good, saved or unsaved; that suffering is
> good for you or something you deserve for being "bad"; and
> that if you are feeling depressed that means that God has
> deserted you and that therefore you must be really bad.
>
> The realization that I am just another primate on this
> earth, that living is all there is to life, that looking at a billboard
> featuring a cute male and lusting after him is not evil, and that
> the world is messed up just because that is the nature of
> humanity and not because of someone's decision to eat an
> apple, are such liberating thoughts that I no longer have any
> negative existential thoughts at all. In fact, since becoming an
> atheist, I have never been happier.

Donna agreed:

> I've suffered from depression since I became an atheist, but in
> general I'm much happier and more emotionally stable, and

I experience more joy and peace now than I ever did as a Christian. What happens to me now is usually that between projects (like when I finish one book and am not ready to start another one), I get spurts of anxiety and depression. But since it's happened repeatedly in my career, it's become predictable and hence less disturbing to me. Now I realize that "this too shall pass," and that thought makes the bad feelings less intense. The down period does not usually last very long once I recognize what's happening.

When I was a Christian I was almost always "going through a wilderness experience," and my emotions were completely volatile. I was ready to go off on a tantrum or into a depression at the slightest provocation. I was also always feeling guilty and anxious because I was trying to live by other people's expectations. Now that I live according to my own conscience, I never feel guilty. I just don't do things that violate my own conscience; I am not holding myself responsible to follow the rules of some book or to act in a way that satisfies someone else's expectations of how I should behave.

Martha described her experience:

I guess I'm just a cockeyed optimist, because I rarely get truly depressed and when I do, I can usually trace it to hormonal wackiness. A lot of the time, I'm so busy with the day-to-day realities of working and taking care of my family and taking part in the world of politics and ideas that I'm too distracted to spend a lot of time contemplating the negative. I did notice that the last few family vacations that we went on (which involved a lot of hanging around and relaxing) brought up some of those existential negative feelings.

I was always a pretty optimistic, contented person when I was a Christian, so I think that it's part of my nature. However, I did have a big cloud of guilt and angst hanging over me because I took original sin so seriously. I keenly felt that I was always falling short and not living the truly victorious Christian life (whatever that was supposed to mean!). Now that I don't have that nonsense in my head any longer and I can make my own decisions without consulting the Bible or God in prayer, I'm much freer. I also speak my mind more and act more honestly in my personal and professional relationships, and that also makes me happier.

So who is more likely to feel blue, believers or atheists? In the absence of experiments based on sound measures, we are left to speculate — and there is every reason to conclude that believers are the more depressed group. One straightforward piece of evidence is that most people in America identify themselves as religious, and antidepressants are the most prescribed medication in America. Who is taking all those antidepressants? While this may not be proof positive, it is certainly suggestive.

THE ATHEIST OPPORTUNITY

Comprehending the facts of existence, including the extent to which the universe is completely indifferent to us, can be depressing (although the activity of making meaning acts as an antidote to that depression). But it is also easy to suppose that fooling yourself into believing that the universe is benevolent, that you and some made-up god have a relationship, that your god felt just fine downing that plane with your football team on it, and so on — that is, trying to live with the impossible contradictions that belief produces — is actually a surer cause of depression.

It is certainly the case, in my experience working as a therapist and coach to thousands of creative and performing artists, that the believers have been the more depressed clients. This is especially true of the sensitive, intelligent believer working on a memoir about his or her "spiritual experiences" — a book that the author often finds impossible to complete. Too truthful to write patent nonsense but too firmly in the grip of god-talk or spirit-talk to make a break for freedom, this author is likely to spend ten years "writing but not really writing" the book, depressed all the while. This experience mirrors the painful inner conflict confronting many believers, since their desire to maintain belief smacks up against impressive reasons for not believing.

Nor is it a depression they tend to understand as they defensively avoid a direct chat with themselves in which they air their doubts. Denying the reality of this inner conflict, they misattribute their experience and decide that they have a disease, the "disease" of depression. Since they have little internal permission to look this depression in the eye and accurately identify its source — just as they have little internal permission to look the universe in the eye   they end up fibbing to themselves about the source of their depression, abdicating responsibility for it, calling it a disease, and accepting their doctor's prescription of antidepressants.

All things considered, it is quite likely the believer — and especially the believer with doubts and scruples — who gets bluer. She is blue because in a corner of her consciousness she knows that the universe is exactly what it is, devoid of gods and disinterested in her. She is also blue because she knows she is maintaining her beliefs in gods against her own better judgment, thereby turning herself into a hypocrite. How can these inner conflicts do anything but bring her down?

As atheists we have the opportunity to be more honest about the blues that we experience. We can say, "My stupid job is making me blue." We can say, "I am filled with despair that the excellent novel I wrote can't seem to find a publisher." We can say, "I am made ineffably sad by the corruption of politicians." We can say, "I feel cheated that this is what life is all about." We can say, "I'm mortified that I'm accomplishing so little." We get to honestly look at the thing itself and not shift the issue to our relationship to some nonexistent god.

The first step in dealing with the blues is to be honest — which, to begin with, may bring us additional pain. Maybe we will discover that the source of our sadness is our alcoholism. Maybe we will discover that our very idea about how to live — as a stockbroker, a volunteer, an emergency room physician, a recluse, a party animal, a weaver, a mogul, a loner — no longer holds sufficient meaning and must be overthrown in favor of a different life. To be honest is to invite realizations of this sort — and a full measure of pain. But it is a necessary first step, the same step we ask of believers when we ask them to look honestly at their faulty belief systems.

We assert that if believers dared to think through the logic of their positions, they would be forced to abandon them. We demand that they think. Therefore we must buy our own argument and agree that we, too, must think, in this case about what causes our case of the blues and what we intend to do to release ourselves from its grip. If we are defensive in this regard and rush to call our sadness a "disease," so as to avoid thinking through what is going on, we are doing exactly what believers do when they rush to accept the existence of gods. God is their easy answer; we don't want "disease" to be our easy answer.

In fact, we have an excellent answer: that we can make meaning. When, as a modern person, you are forced to mentally wrestle with issues like mass starvation, global warming, the privatization of scarce resources, and torture televised into your living room, it is not surprising that you despair. But that we despair sometimes does not mean that we must allow believers to tar us with the false charge that we are more depressed than they. They are courting a much more serious depression by holding on to erroneous beliefs and knowing that they should not.

CHAPTER SEVEN

We Deal with Meaninglessness

(Yes, by Making Meaning)

Atheism is not just the belief that god-talk is human-made folderol and that gods, like unicorns, do not exist. It is a complete worldview. An atheist looks at the world and sees certain facts of existence. He sees that he is the product of sightless nature and not of a watchful mind. He sees that he is embodied and enlivened in a certain way and for a certain amount of time: if you cut out his brain, he will cease to be. He knows that his identity and sense of self exist only as long as his brain remains intact — pierce his brain with a lance, and he may suddenly fancy himself a tap dancer or a financier.

Most fundamentally, he understands that, when he says that he lives and then he dies, he is saying something about his essential freedom and his equally real despair. He is free to live his life, but he is not spared the pain of recognizing his predicament as a passing thing. That freedom he uses to make meaning. That pain arrives as meaninglessness. On many days he may experience both: the sense that he has made some meaning and the pain of meaninglessness.

Here is a dramatic but straightforward example of this dynamic tension at play. You are about to be executed because the powers that be have decided to execute everyone with brown eyes. You are in a prison camp for brown-eyed people and you have calculated, based on your observations, that tomorrow it will be your turn to die. How will you approach your fate? You might experience it as personally meaningful to walk into the oven with your head held high; or to try to take out one guard; or to smile and tell a joke; or to help your neighbor, who has grown hysterical. You might construe many actions and attitudes as meaningful in this situation, ones that would make you proud of yourself.

At the same time, you understand perfectly well that you are about to be rendered permanently gone and that whatever gesture you make or attitude you adopt is a small, meaningless thing that doesn't affect your oppressors and doesn't save your life. You may manage to make yourself feel proud, because you are comporting yourself exactly as you intend, but you will also despair, because you know that your attitude, as commendable as it may be, is also pointless. In that split second personal meaning and personal meaninglessness coexist, creating a feeling with no name that is a mixture of mile-wide sadness and mile-deep pride.

Let's continue with a more everyday example. You wake up one Saturday morning enthusiastic to buy a filing cabinet so that you can organize the notes for the novel that you are writing. You drive to the mall, energized because this little expedition is in the service of your meaning-making needs. At the mall, you start to sink a little. You recognize that not a soul you are passing is a member of the audience for your novel. The thought begins to percolate in your brain that you are wasting your time writing a novel that precious few people will read.

You find the right filing cabinet; but you already don't care. It costs considerably more money than you had intended to pay, but if you don't buy it, your day will feel even more meaningless, so you buy it. Now two bad feelings begin to eat at you: that you just spent an extravagant amount of money on a filing cabinet for a book that no one will want and also that your meaning path is a ridiculous one and that you really should have gone to law school or taken over the family business. By the time you get home from the mall with your filing cabinet, filing is the next-to-last thing on your mind (writing your novel is the last thing). Pouring a very tall Scotch is the first. How far are you from a depression, an anxiety attack, or an addictive binge? Not very.

In the above example, you started the day with some good meaning-making intentions, and then a drop of meaninglessness ended up poisoning the day. But what if you had started the day without any solid meaning-making intentions? What if you'd gotten up that Saturday morning and, instead of turning to the writing of your novel, you let some doubts about your talent or some anxiety about not knowing how to proceed with your current chapter interfere with your meaning-making intentions? Rather than face this small crisis and reinvest meaning in your novel, which would have led to a productive and possibly satisfying day, you allow the big sale at the mall to pop into your head, get falsely excited, and rush off to buy some things that you already know you don't need.

You know what happens next. You proceed with mock

enthusiasm for several hours, buy some sale items, have lunch, shop a little more in worsening humor and, with diminishing energy, make it home exhausted, lay out the things you purchased, realize that you do not want any of them, go to bed sad and defeated, and, to compound the fiasco, spend the next day, Sunday, again not working on your novel as you wait in line to return the items you bought the day before. You will have experienced your weekend as a sojourn in meaninglessness.

In the first scenario, a meaning crisis occurred while you were engaged in a meaningful activity (getting that filing cabinet). In the second scenario, the meaning crisis occurred earlier in the day (when you doubted your ability to handle your novel) and caused you to conjure up a meaning substitute (shopping at a mall sale). Here is a third open door for the experience of meaninglessness to enter: you wake up not knowing where or how to make meaning and with the sense that another dreary day awaits you. In this scenario, meaninglessness dogs your heels and colors your day from the moment you awaken.

You plan your day as you do every day, listing one boring thing after another and not giving in to your inclination to pull the covers over your head. Eventually you dart off to the mall to shop. You shop, you come home, you put away your purchases, you do the next thing and the next on your list — knowing in your heart that you have failed at what you perceive as a fundamental human task, discerning what matters. Tomorrow your list will look similar and your day will feel similar, shrouded in meaninglessness.

Janet, a poet, related her experience:

> Once in the middle of a very long period of unhappiness, my husband asked me as we were turning the corner toward our home of fifteen years, "What kind of car do you want next?"

The question struck me speechless. A whole zoo of feelings began to slither inside me. In the context of my years of struggle and my feelings of hopelessness about change, his question seemed just so inane. I suddenly realized that he probably could have asked me any similar question — "What do you want for Christmas?" or "Where would you like to go on vacation?" — and the utter meaninglessness not just of the question but of my life would similarly have been revealed.

Fran, a painter, added:

> Meaninglessness is an inescapable part of our modern culture. Midlife crisis. Adolescent angst. Postcollege blues. All these things are essentially meaninglessness events and exist as a consequence of existing in our production-oriented, industrial, consumerist culture. We work to produce money and we wonder what we are doing. Our consumerist economic climate gives us a solution: buy, buy, and buy some more. We are told that's the solution to our problems. But sooner or later, we find out that it isn't. Then where are we?

Countless people suffer from meaning crises. They've gotten a whiff of meaninglessness and don't know where to turn to find meaning. If they land on any answer, it is often in the territory of the supernatural: they imagine that their best bet is to renew their faith, switch churches, consult a psychic, pull out a Tarot deck, keep kosher, confess, atone, pray harder. But all that proves cold comfort. In his book *Existential Psychotherapy*, existential psychotherapist Irvin Yalom used the following anonymous suicide note as an epigraph to a chapter on meaninglessness. The despairing suicide wrote:

> Imagine a happy group of morons who are engaged in work. They are carrying bricks in an open field. As soon as they've

stacked all the bricks at one end of the field, they proceed to transport them to the opposite end. This continues without stop. Every day of every year they are busy doing the same thing. One day one of the morons stops long enough to ask himself what he is doing. He wonders what purpose there is in carrying the bricks. And from that instant on he is not quite as content with his occupation as he had been before. I am the moron who wonders why he is carrying the bricks.[1]

This visceral experience of meaninglessness, of being a moron carrying bricks, causes a person to need good reasons to go on, reasons that can counteract the despair of meaninglessness. If these reasons can't be discerned, a meaning crisis occurs. How many people have encountered the despair of meaninglessness and not found an antidote? Viktor Frankl, a meaning-oriented psychotherapist like Yalom, provided some suggestive numbers. In one study, he reported an incidence rate for an "existential vacuum" of 81 percent for American college students.[2] In his own investigations, Yalom found that 30 percent of his subjects had "some major problem involving meaning." Who today hasn't gotten a good whiff of meaninglessness — and come up with too few good answers?

I am presenting the case that you can counteract this experience of existential vacuum, this whiff of meaninglessness, and these meaning problems by deciding that you will invest meaning and by then investing it. You decide to care. You decide to be passionate. You decide that this relationship matters or that that work matters. Does it matter to Martians or Venutians? No. But you decide that it matters to you, that according to your understanding of how your life is to be lived, this is a meaningful relationship to cultivate or a meaningful job to undertake. You adopt making meaning as the centerpiece strategy of your life, and you know exactly what to do when meaninglessness strikes.

Human beings have always had the potential to know meaninglessness. Modern times activated that potential. We call this the modern period because of the profound changes wrought on the species by increased scientific understanding, paradigm shifts in the way we view the universe, and progress in the direction of an enlightened regard for the individual. It's not even mildly strange that advances in scientific understanding and a heightened valuation of the individual have provoked a culture-wide explosion of meaninglessness. You can't peer behind the curtain and spot all the cogs and wheels, you can't inflate the individual and give her outlandish hope while leaving her life-size and all too human, you can't make her carry bricks and not create a meaninglessness epidemic.

Martha, an art professor, shared her story:

> I have experienced meaninglessness most of my life. I always thought it was simply depression and had no idea that it could be more than depression or other than depression. Meaninglessness is soul destroying; it sucks the life right out of you. It literally feels like "nothing matters" and "there's no good reason to live" and "why bother?" And it's all the more exquisitely painful because no one else in my environment ever seems to feel that way — or rather, those who do (usually women) are written off by everyone (including me) as "hysterics" and "neurotics" not worth bothering with. I am just thrilled to have this new framework, that I must make meaning, and that I can stop waiting for some miracle of meaning to happen!

Meaninglessness can leap to the foreground at any time, causing a meaning crisis and a real depression. On the atheist's way, you meet this poignant problem by making all the meaning you need. Meaning is a completely renewable resource. Naturally, there are countless other ways to handle our painful knowledge about our lot: by drinking, by drowning in material goods, by drawing the blinds, by making the supernatural error. All these methods are inferior to making meaning.

AVOIDING THE SUPERNATURAL ERROR

One of these inferior methods interests us particularly: dealing with recurrent meaninglessness by making the supernatural error. The supernatural error is that of mislabeling the source of a personal experience (like a feeling of awe) or an event in the world (like a beautiful sunset) as being of supernatural origin when the source is simply natural. Billions of people commit this error — and take pride in its commission. It is a prime pillar of belief and a common mechanism for dealing with the stark facts of existence.

If you announce to yourself that the gorgeous sunset directly in front of you is god's handiwork, you have instantly created a pleasing picture that includes a lovely place in it for you. If, on the other hand, you tell yourself the truth, that this loveliness is the product of five-alarm pollution, you have opened the door to feelings of despair. Is it any wonder that many people look at a sunset and smile — at the comforting fantasy about beneficent gods that they have just produced in their own minds?

We enjoy the fragrance of a rose and conjure gods: that is an example of the supernatural error. We are amazed by the lushness of our garden and announce that we have had a spiritual experience: that is an example of the supernatural error. We look up at the night sky, see a million stars and feel awestruck, and imagine that we have unraveled some eternal mystery: that is an example of the supernatural error. The rose's fragrance, the garden's lushness, and the night sky's grandeur affect us because we are built to appreciate beauty and to experience awe. To leap to a supernatural source for these powerful but ordinary feelings is to indulge in wishful thinking, romantic embellishment, and metaphoric fantasizing.

Fran, a member of my online atheism group, offered the following thoughts:

> The things about our universe that we have yet to understand aren't supernatural, just natural. As a society and as a species we are in the throes of outgrowing God as an explanation for what we don't yet understand. How far back in history do we need to go before cell phones would have been considered "supernatural"? Or computers, nanotechnology, organ transplants — you name it?
>
> I'm no historian or scientist, but it seems obvious to me that the concept of God was developed in an effort to explain realities that science explains and explores today. The more we can understand the natural workings of the universe, the less we need God to explain them. Unfortunately, turning to supernatural explanations is easy   and, for billions of people, it is their default way of explaining every powerful or unusual thing that they encounter, including their own feelings.

Leslie echoed these ideas:

> There is no need to invoke the supernatural or the concept of a deity to treasure experiences that inspire awe, wonder, timelessness, poignancy, a sense of commonality with other people, or a feeling of one's connections within a larger web of life. If we just try, we can maintain a healthy perspective that recognizes both our insignificance on a cosmic scale and our potentially enormous significance within our human communities and on the scale at which we lead our lives.
>
> We can maintain an attitude of reverence and mindfulness

and an appreciation for phenomena that are awe inspiring or ineffable without a need to insist that everything have an immediately accessible explanation. It's important to recognize that these experiences are real — and that they don't have to be attributed to supernatural causes.

You might think of the supernatural error as a naming error: you see a wisp of fog and, feeling a bit anxious and having a head full of ghost stories, you call it a ghost. Or you might think of the supernatural error as an attribution error: having no understanding of science, you analogize from the way your tribe wars with its neighboring tribes and attribute the wildness of storms to the warring of gods. Or you might think of it as a formal fallacy: illogically moving from one class of things (like the scent of flowers) to a qualitatively different class of things (like the landscape of heaven).

However you define it, the supernatural error is a prime way that people attempt to spare themselves uncomfortable and painful feelings. The fog doesn't make them see ghosts; it is an internal mechanism, an inclination of the psyche, a predisposition to fantasy and easy metaphor that conjures a ghost out of moist air. As John, a lawyer, put it, "This labeling error occurs in people who *already* harbor a belief in supernatural phenomena. People who already believe in an immaterial, immortal soul, in chi or chakras or astral planes, and so on, are that much more ready to take an intense wordless experience and cite it as evidence of something supernatural or spiritual."

Why do people feel so comfortable committing this error? For a variety of reasons having to do with how the brain works. One important reason is our evolved ability to spot patterns — even when they don't exist. If I believe in ghosts, then I will see a ghost in a wisp of fog, in a shadow flitting across the wall, and in the draperies moving in a soft breeze. My conviction that ghosts exist is confirmed because I see a pattern of ghostly activity.

Don, a software designer, elaborated on this phenomenon:

> The human brain is very good at spotting patterns. This is a survival technique. If you can look at an overhanging tree branch and spot the python coiled around the branch, even though you only see little bits of two or three coils, you're more likely to survive. So, say that you're lying in your lounger staring at an expanse of wallpaper on which an entirely random bunch of paint daubs have been splattered. If you stare for a minute or two you are going to start to see a rabbit, or a clown with his head bent, or a three-legged buffalo, or whatever. Analogously, if you believe in God, there's a very high probability that you will encounter several events each day that seem to provide firm evidence that "God is working in your life." The pattern-spotter in you is processing the random noise in your life and producing what appears to be a pattern. That's the rabbit-in-the-wallpaper effect!

Another reason that committing the supernatural error is so common is that it allows for what has been dubbed "premature closure," that is, the quick (but too quick) solution to a problem that provokes anxiety and causes cognitive dissonance. As Mark, a sculptor, put it, "Premature closure is the shutting off of a full exploration of the possible meanings of a new experience because we unconsciously fear that a full exploration might be too painful or dangerous. A person has an inexplicable experience of the mystical variety and then rushes to put it in a familiar category in order to 'understand' it. The problem is handled quickly and effortlessly — but illegitimately."

What dangers are associated with committing the supernatural error? One profound one is that repeatedly making this
error acts like Novocain on the brain. You take a walk in your garden, decide that you've had a spiritual experience, feel as if you've
actually accomplished something — you've had a spiritual experience, after all! — and, with that sense of accomplishment in your
pocket, find yourself that much less ready to make the meaning
you might have made if you hadn't just anaesthetized yourself.

A second profound danger is the way the error generalizes
and causes you to make false distinctions and create unreasoned
categories. Falling prey to this inclination, you begin to label
certain activities as "soulful" and other activities as "soulless."
You may even organize your whole life around these error-
ridden distinctions and decide to become a nun, or a past-lives
regression therapist. Or you may regret your decision to choose
a "practical" profession and lament not having taken a more
"spiritual" path. In this way the error begins to permeate and taint
everything.

Even the metaphor of "seeking meaning" is a version of the
supernatural error. There is no meaning to *find*. There is only the
meaning we *make*. Meaning is a choice, not a lost object. If you
are a believer, you must make your meaning too, since no religion
posits that it is the business of gods to tell you to become a doctor
or a lawyer or to go to war or refrain from fighting. If you are not
a believer, you have an even clearer mandate. There is nothing and
no one to tell you how to live or why to live. Either you make your
meaning, or meaninglessness swallows you up.

Right now, at this moment in our evolution, meaninglessness
is a scourge that is implicated in our depression epidemic, our insomnia epidemic, and all our undiagnosed disorders of meaning.

But the meaninglessness we are experiencing to a record degree may turn out to be nothing more than the prime feature of a two-century period of adjustment. Our great-grandchildren may look back on our struggles with meaninglessness as a signal marker in the long movement from despair to matter-of-fact heroism in the face of the facts of existence. By then, the idea that meaning must be made may have become the reigning intellectual paradigm. Let us continue our movement in that direction, by avoiding all supernatural errors and by dealing with meaning in this new way, as available as our next breath or our next heartbeat.

CHAPTER EIGHT

We Choose Our Meanings

(Or Do They Choose Us?)

In suggesting that a person living the atheist's way must consciously and passionately make meaning, I am asking that she engage in a paradigm shift in the direction of more mindful, serious action, increased attention to the moral and existential spheres, and a better effort at manifesting her freedom: from dogma and from her own defenses. To demand that she manifest her freedom in these ways is of course to presume that she is able to do so. This is an age-old debate — to what extent are we free, and to what extent are we determined? — and the answer matters.

The idea that we can make meaning and force life to mean what we intend it to mean implies, to begin with, that we are in charge of our motives, aware of our inner workings, larger than our primitive cravings, and clear-eyed about life's realities and challenges. But are we in charge, aware, large enough, and clear-eyed? Since we witness people doing so many things that are not in their self-interest, like becoming morbidly obese and bringing on their own diabetes or smoking themselves into emphysema and lung cancer, it's hard to believe that people know themselves or are in control of their actions. Is making meaning within our grasp, a pipe dream, or even a logical impossibility?

It's clear why we have serious doubts. How many people pick their mate for shadowy reasons having nothing to do with suitability? How many opt for limiting tribal identities of place, race, or belief and turn the world into a battlefield? How many interact poorly with their parents or their children, even though they've had decades to alter that dynamic? How many are preoccupied with the latest gossip and other trivial matters? Aren't there millions upon millions in each category?

We are right to have serious doubts about whether we human beings are equal to the challenge of making meaning. We seem too much at the mercy of our instincts, too much like slaves to our unconscious motives and yearnings, too affected by our primitive brains, too existentially unaware and too handcuffed by our constructed personalities to step up to the meaning plate. If we possess such a limited amount of freedom that to even call it freedom is a romantic stretch, then my entire program is a lovely fraud, something like advising a mouse with aspirations that he really can become a lion. Are we as trapped and limited as that?

Nor are those internal constraints the only sources of our doubt about the possibility of freedom. What if you are employed in a job so meaningless that meaning could not be made there even if you applied all the effort in the world? What if you must care for a chronically ill child whose needs drain your energy? What if you dream of investing meaning in playing basketball but are short, slow, and uncoordinated? What if you dream of investing meaning in singing opera but you have no range or pitch? What if, because your family was poor, you had all your teeth extracted at once as a way to cure your dental problems, so that now you wear bad false teeth that keep you in constant pain? How can you make meaning while in misery?

In short, what about the freedom-reducing bite of reality? What if you are imprisoned? What if the career you love has become obsolete? What if you find yourself old and infirm? What if an invading army suddenly occupies your neighborhood? What if food and water become scarce and survival is the only thing on your mind? What if your investments turn to ash? What if you lose a child and feel your heart break? What if you find yourself in a dead-end job with a family to support and a rope of debt around your neck?

We could try to rationalize away each of these lacks of freedom. We could call our jail cell our sanctuary. We could call our chronic pain the way that we are tested, the way we are made stronger. We could talk ourselves into reporting on basketball, rather than playing it, or regularly attending the opera, rather than singing it, and assert that being this close to our love is meaning enough. We could claim that our old age has brought with it wisdom and that our infirmity is the opportunity we've been seeking to slow down and smell the roses. It is a special talent of our species to rationalize, and we might rationalize away the ferocious bite of reality.

Say that you're a painter who can't afford to buy expensive pigments. Grudgingly you settle for cheap ones. Then, in order to stay mentally balanced, you rationalize. You turn your lemons into lemonade. You reframe the matter as a test of your artistic abilities and as an opportunity for heroism. You say, "These cheap pigments have virtues that I intend to understand." You say, "This will make me a stronger painter." You create the illusion — the adaptive illusion, we are tempted to say — that you are doing just fine. That was van Gogh's solution to this exact predicament. Among his many problems was the high cost of pigments. He couldn't afford the pigments he wanted and turned the sourness of poverty into lemonade by adding the sugar of precedent. He wrote to his brother, Theo, his paint supplier, "In case you should be a bit hard up, I could manage perfectly without the expensive blues and the carmine. One tube of Prussian blue yields as much as six tubes of ultramarine or cobalt and costs six times less. Delacroix swore by that vulgar blue and used it often."[1]

Did van Gogh believe his own rationalizations? Can we successfully deal with the freedom-reducing bite of reality by rationalizing away every difficulty, by finding some sugar for every lemon, by asserting that a lack of freedom is the illusion and that we can contrive a sense of freedom out of any set of circumstances? Isn't this exactly what we do when we proclaim that we are not pointless, disposable energy packets but rather valuable creatures? Isn't the one god we really need Maya, the Hindu goddess of illusion? Isn't it a brilliant policy to create these adaptive illusions and then fervently believe them, even though we know that we ourselves created them?

The answer is the same one that I offered previously: just as you are the only one identified by nature to arbitrate meaning in your life, you are also the only one in a position to judge whether or not you have sufficient freedom to make meaning. You must answer this question only for you — and not for the vast multitude. If the throngs are not free, that poses a tremendous problem for all of us, since their lack of freedom endangers us all. But if you are not free, the game is over. So what is your best guess? Are the bite of reality and the pull of your impulses such freedom-reducing constraints that you face life in a prison cell? Or are you free enough to orchestrate the meaning in your life?

You might come to an answer something like the following, provided by Frank, a corporate manager:

> We feel that we have free will. No one disputes that. But the sources of the decisions that we make are partly (or entirely) unconscious and are ultimately beyond our control. Our unconscious mental processes operate automatically, and they dictate what we will do. Ultimately, making the choice between, say, eating a cheeseburger and eating a green salad boils down to this: Which mental process will win some invisible, multifaceted internal arm-wrestling contest? The mental and emotional weight given to my various choices is, at root, an automatic process. That's why alcoholics drink themselves to death: the craving is stronger than the fear, and they have no control over the relative weights of those two mental processes.
>
> In some circumstances I can get in there and try to manipulate the mental weighting process. For example, I may sign up for a weight-loss class, which may tilt the scales in favor of the salad. But again, I ultimately have no control over whether I sign up for the weight-loss class, because that decision is made unconsciously, based on the same kinds of complex emotional weighing and balancing. If you follow through this process of analysis with some kind of rigor, I suspect that you'll find, as the Buddhists say, that there's "nobody home." The universe is just going through this incredibly complex process, and there is no "you" outside the process who is intimately aware of it and can direct it. Free will is a useful illusion for natural selection to foster, because it encourages us to weigh our options carefully, and that has a positive

survival value. But the weighing process itself depends on unconscious, automatic factors.

Frank's answer is characteristic of the debate between free will and determinism. We know that at least some of the time we experience what feels like free will, but we also suspect that even that limited amount of felt freedom — to opt for this career rather than that one or to choose as our mate this person rather than that one — may be a chimera. We suspect that motives zipping around out of conscious awareness have compelled us to make this particular choice and then provided us with reasons to justify it, reasons that sound persuasive enough to our own ears that we can nod and exclaim, "Yes, I chose this!" This may be nature's exact game.

Still, we are creatures who can comment on our situation as eloquently as Frank did. This reasoned eloquence makes us pause. As constrained as we are, maybe we are just barely free enough. Maybe you find yourself saying something like the following to yourself: "Well, yes, I am pretty shadowy to myself, and yes, I steal the occasional cigarette, and yes, I know that I make some of my own troubles by the way I let myself wallow in the past, and yes, I can sense the hundred ways that I am tossed and turned and infinitely less free than I would like to be, but still, damn it all, I know that I bring more than occasional awareness to the table and that I can be the instrument of my own fate!" That amount of freedom, the freedom you just articulated, will do for now. Let's call that "freedom enough." We have not answered the free will–determinism question, but we have decided to come down on the side of personal freedom, to assert it whether or not it exists. Just as we make our own meaning, we make our own freedom. If this is a cosmic joke, then let us be the ones laughing.

PROVING THE EXCEPTION

The amount of freedom that we are presuming is available to you is freedom enough to permit you to cultivate additional self-awareness, if you choose to make meaning of that sort. It is freedom enough to allow you to introduce a regular practice into your life, like writing for an hour each day or being of service for an hour each day, if you choose to make meaning of that sort. It is freedom enough to get a picture in your mind of your life as a never-ending project, if you choose to make meaning of that sort. It is freedom enough to open the door a crack to greater freedom — even to push the door wide open — if you choose to make meaning of that sort.

It may not be complete or exceptional freedom, but it is enough freedom that you can prove the exception. The first choice on your agenda is to choose between proving the rule and proving the exception, an idea that is a cousin to the idea of nominating yourself as the maker of meaning in your life. Billions of people may not be free enough to let go of their made-up gods. You will not allow that sad fact to prevent you from proving the exception. Billions of people may not be equal to seeing beyond limited self-interest to a more mindful self-interest that takes into account the future of the species. You will not allow that sad fact to prevent you from proving the exception. The amount of freedom you are claiming for yourself allows you to affirm the following remarkable thing: "I will prove the exception!"

To live the atheist's way, you must opt to use the freedom you possess, whatever its exact amount and however it may be construed, to prove the exception. Naturally, the "must" in that sentence is a bit of authorial silliness; you can live your life any way you want. No one is in charge of your life but you, and you can sun yourself from morning until night, or make a merciless fortune, or memorize the statistics of your sports teams. You are in charge of your life. If, however, you have been reading along and nodding, if you recognize that the plan for authentic living that I'm describing matches your aspirations and suits your purposes, then you will want to step to the plate as the exception, as someone who minimizes rote, reflexive behavior and maximizes reasoned behavior.

Countless models have been postulated to explain why we do what we do. Freud developed his model of the tripartite psyche made up of id, ego, and superego, articulated ideas about the unconscious and the defenses, and created a view of a mechanical person driven by sexual energy. Jung altered the Freudian model by adding a collective unconscious, introducing religious-tinged archetypes, and arguing that, rather than developing over time, we come out whole and then subsequently shrink, losing parts of ourselves until, dazed and confused, we experience the famous midlife crisis. Adler argued that we are primarily driven by our need to compensate for our shortcomings and our weaknesses. These three models join the scores of others — and their million elaborations — that speculators on our condition have cut out of whole cloth.

Here is our simple model, no worse and no better than the models postulated in the past. It will serve us nicely as we explore making meaning and living the atheist's way. Imagine that our choices are sometimes a matter of indifference, sometimes a matter of instinct, and sometimes a matter of intention. In the first two instances we are chosen, so to speak, acting in rote and reflexive ways, and in the third instance we choose, using our freedom and our reason. I am holding a belief in gods as one of those rote and reflexive things and atheism as a reasoned thing, but the model applies to every aspect of human existence.

These categories reflect our common-sense experiences of life. To begin with, much that we do is a matter of indifference to us. Sometimes it is actually our personality style to go through the motions mechanically, uttering rote greetings in certain situations, doing a certain sort of work when we find ourselves at our desks, eating a certain sort of lunch because it is our habit. Many people have this look and feel to them: they seem defined by the fact that no one is at home. Other people arrive at rote living through crisis and catastrophe, going through the motions because they feel depressed, trapped, defeated, injured, or grief-stricken.

Often we live indifferently. At other times we are driven by our instincts and desires, by the pull to wolf down a ham sandwich, by the urge to follow that attractive stranger, by the demands of our pleasure center, by the force of some complicated psychological explosion that causes us to treat the next person we meet cruelly. Call this the roiling Freudian id, name it our lizard or leopard brain, describe it in terms of mechanisms like fight-or-flight, analogize to the tropisms displayed by plants: it is a phenomenon we each know personally. It fills our dreams with demons, surprises us by its power and its grip, and makes us wonder why in heaven's name we just did what we did. We know all about those reflexes and instincts.

However, they don't define us. Our instincts may push us toward an addiction. We can still form the intention to live soberly. Our instincts may incline us toward a full day of watching television. We can still form the intention to forgo that ease and engage in more meaningful activity. It may be a reflexive defense to feel insulted when we are told a hard truth, but we can still form the intention to appreciate that truth. We spend too much time moving mechanically through life, and we are driven like a harnessed animal by our instincts, but still we possess an inner eye of reason and the power to shine a beacon light of reason everywhere, on ourselves and on our world.

This light of reason is the bright light we shine on life so that we can see it clearly. It is not a "right-brain" or "left-brain" sort of thing, not a distinction between logic and intuition that inclines toward logic, but rather the way that we use our whole brain and our complete endowment to illuminate our inner landscape, so that we can fathom our motives, and to illuminate our outer landscape, to see how and where reality is biting. It is an attitude of mind and a way of being that serves us as a lighthouse serves mariners: it lights our way. And it requires constant effort, because our eye of reason wants to shut when our desires are activated. To keep it open, we must intend to keep it open and be practiced at keeping it open.

If reason is its own kind of myth, it is the myth we adopt. In an interview with Bill Moyers, Joseph Campbell expressed his desire for new myths that would serve this perilous present. Moyers wondered where these new myths might come from and what they might contain. Campbell replied, "The ground of that new mythology is already here: it is the eye of reason, not of my nationality; the eye of reason, not of my religious community; the eye of reason, not of my linguistic community. And this could be the philosophy for the whole planet, not just for this group, that group, or the other group. When you see the earth from the moon, you don't see any divisions of nations or states. The eye of reason might be the symbol for the new mythology to come."[2]

You answer each challenge in a reasoned way. In some circumstances, the answer is, "I can change this, and I must change this." If your work is unbearable, this is what you say. If you are morbidly obese, this is what you say. In other circumstances, the answer is, "I will make the best of this." If you are in chronic pain that just can't be relieved, this is what you say. If you have responsibilities that can't be avoided, this is what you say. This is a familiar version of the message that sensible men and women have been delivering since the dawn of the species. Reality hammers us hard, manifesting as wars and stock market crashes, as addictions and sudden panics. We prove the exception not by wresting control of the universe but by making a certain demand on ourselves, that we will shine the light of reason on life and act accordingly.

Where we can affect the situation by our actions, we take those actions. Where we can affect the situation by our attitude, we take charge of our attitude. What we do not do is give in or give up. I am not underestimating the extent to which reality plays havoc with the idea of making meaning. I am giving reality its due. I am saying something simple and incontrovertible: you are obliged to do what you can. Never made it as a movie star? Then make meaning in some other way. Not pleased with the person you see in the mirror? Change. Feel trapped by a hornet's nest of circumstances, from your credit card debt to your childhood limp to your lack of success? You know the answer. Apply the light of reason to each of these circumstances, change what can be changed, do what must be done — and make yourself proud.

CHAPTER NINE

We Make Idiosyncratic Meaning Choices

(As Is Our Right and Obligation)

Now that we have decided that we will prove the exception, what comes next? How do we proceed to make meaning? What criteria do we use to predict that some activity or endeavor is going to feel meaningful? How do we judge whether what we have undertaken is actually meeting our meaning needs? How often can we allow ourselves to indulge in rote or reflexive behavior, and how often must we strive to make meaning? In short, how does making meaning work? You know one part of the answer: no god is going to tell you.

There is the story of the farmer who was informed that an art collector had paid a very handsome price for a painting of the farmer's barn. The farmer exclaimed, "For that price he could have had the whole farm!" It is exactly and quintessentially human to pay more for a painting of a barn than for the farm itself. For the collector, the painting holds meaning: it is evocative, it is beautiful, it reminds him of nature, there is no tilling and planting to bother with, and he expects that it will appreciate nicely. This is our strange territory, the territory of idiosyncratic meaning.

You have decided to make meaning. You have nominated yourself as the hero of your own story. Now what? One sort of question has been answered: you know what attitude you will adopt with respect to the universe. You will stand up and be counted, even though only you are doing the counting. But an endless series of questions remains unanswered. Exactly what meaning will you make? What meaning will you make after lunch today, or tomorrow, or on Saturday, or a week from Tuesday? How do you move from a rock-solid attitude to some clear plan of action?

First, let's recall who must do this deciding. A meaning question arises. You wonder if you ought to continue at your job. You wonder if your relationship serves you. You have serious doubts about your latest choices. Where will you turn for an answer? Not to a workshop. Not to an astrologer. Not to a rabbi. Not to your best friend. Not to a psychic. Not to the top book on your pile of reading. You face yourself and you provide yourself with your own best answers.

For in the realm of meaning, you must look to your own answers. Doing anything else amounts to a bad habit, existentially speaking. You may not be in a position to diagnose your rash or to know if you have written an effective contract. These are questions that can be answered only by trained experts. But if it is a question of meaning, that is where you take center stage. You are the dancer — and the choreographer. It is time to pose your own questions and then to answer them.

It has become very popular to say, "I may not know the answer, but I'm asking the right question." Often it sounds as if the speaker is not actually interested in the answers and is happy enough not to stand for anything. "We don't know how to fix our school system, but we are asking some really good questions." Actually, we want and need answers. We want them especially with respect to our meaning questions. It is not enough that you ask yourself pertinent questions. That is a vital first step but not the end of the matter.

You must engage in your own analysis, identifying your desires and weighing them against your duties as you construe them. You decide what you love and what you hate; you decide which are worthy actions and which are unworthy; you decide what to value, how to rank those values, and how to integrate those ranked values into a life plan. Is telling truth to power your highest value and your most cherished principle? Then you might nominate yourself an investigative reporter. Is leading a life of words your fiercest desire, and is battling injustice a preeminent value? You might nominate yourself a political novelist. It is of no import what other people consider meaningful, either historically or right now. You must decide.

What are your meaning possibilities? Anything and everything under the sun! Anything can seem meaningful to someone. For Joe, who fancies himself an aristocrat born in the wrong century, it might be his snuffbox collection. For Laura, who grew up in a world of harm, it might be cutting herself: nothing seems more meaningful than feeling alive; and only when the razor cuts her skin does she momentarily wake up. For Bob, it might be following his sports team at home and on the road, spending a small portion of his father's millions to live and die with his team's fortunes.

For Jill it might be looking good: she finds meaning in shopping, in haircuts, in skin creams, in flirting and attracting.

These, however, are unaware meanings, and we will not settle for them. We won't let ourselves feel aristocratic without debating the value of that privileged self-identification. We won't allow cutting ourselves to serve as our best method for feeling alive. That a thing can feel meaningful doesn't mean that we have consciously chosen it, that it actually serves our interests, or that it matches our cherished values. There are an infinite number of meaning possibilities, but only a fraction of them will appeal to someone actively striving to fashion personal meaning.

When we choose the atheist's way, we use our freedom to step back and make conscious decisions that match both our desires and our ethics and that are untangled from primitive or psychological motives. Finding your snuffbox collection, your self-mutilation habits, your team's winning streak, or your reflection in the mirror meaningful is not the same as making meaning. Unprocessed meanings like these arise when we aren't mindful, and they remain in place as long as we avoid self-scrutiny. The hero you intend to be looks in the mirror and sheds every unprocessed meaning she can until, beautifully alert, she stands ready to actually *make* meaning in her life.

To repeatedly behave cruelly, because you were humiliated as a child and now find it satisfying to destroy the people you meet, may be your way. Since the universe does not arbitrate meaning, that option is available to you. But that is a slavish way locked in place by brute psychology. It does not rise to the noble status of making meaning. If on a test you were asked to identify the meaning in your life, you would answer, "Harm people and get even," and you would pass the test. But you would fail our test, the one that requires you to make use of your freedom, however limited it may be, to grow aware, to do better, and to rise higher.

You use your available freedom to step back and make conscious meaning decisions rather than primitive or psychological meaning decisions. You opt for value and not reward; you make value-based and not reward-based meaning decisions. That is the righteous and heroic thing to do and the way that you make yourself proud. How you do this is the art of making meaning. You grow aware any way you like, by thinking, by reflecting, by walking in a tight circle while holding a certain intention, but whatever your tactic, you know to *do* something: self-awareness will not simply happen of its own accord.

One strategy is to create a life purpose statement that comes as close as possible to announcing your overarching meaning intentions. I have discussed the process of creating a statement of this sort in *Coaching the Artist Within* and in *The Van Gogh Blues* and have been gratified to hear that people found this strategy useful.[1] Here is the life purpose statement that Joan, a painter, created and sent to me: "I will triumph over the evil that was done to me, which gave me false limitations. I will participate in loving relationships. I will live well and make a meaningful life by working hard to become the best painter I can be, through drawing and painting five or six days a week." Marcia, a singer-songwriter, actively trying to manage her mood swings and her stress, riffed on the word *instrument*: "My instrument is tuned for the world to move through me. I care for my instrument to keep it tuned. I take care in how I place my instrument in the world."

Your life purpose statement may be a word long, a sentence long, a paragraph long, or a page long. A heartwarming example of using this process came from an elementary school teacher. At the beginning of the school year she explained to her young students the idea of existential responsibility. Then she took them to a nearby stream to gather stones, provided them with craft paints and brushes, and had them inscribe their individual stone with their (very abbreviated) life purpose statement. The students kept their stones on their desks the whole school year. She reported that they were much more able to self-regulate and to focus on their work because of this reminder about the meaning they intended to make.

Having a life purpose statement in place reminds you of the sorts of meaning investments you intend to make and helps you know where to spend your capital and how to realize your potential. However, creating such a statement is just a tactic. A life purpose statement is not a substitute for continually practicing self-awareness and monitoring the meaning issues in your life. When you commit to active meaning-making, you agree to participate in a lifetime adventure of deciding where to make meaning investments, with respect both to the next hour and to the meaning questions that arise over time.

How do you know if you've created the appropriate life purpose statement or landed on a right understanding of the meaning issues in your life? There is no way to know. You decide; you live your decision; you monitor your decision; you reaffirm your decision by reinvesting meaning in your chosen path; you change your mind and make new meaning investments. You take your best stab at deciding what principles you want to manifest and how you intend to marry desire with duty, and then you test your decision in the crucible of life, engaging in trial-and-error experimentation that is the sine qua non of science. We respect science because it tests its hypotheses. We respect ourselves when we do the same.

THE MEANING OF BIRDS

Let's say that you do the work I've been describing. You ascertain what you consider most meaningful in life. You look at your results, feel confident that you have done a decent job of identifying where you want to make meaning, and discover that you aren't at all sure what to do next. What you notice is that the world is not set up to help you translate your idiosyncratic life purposes into real-world activities that match your meaning needs or that provide a living. Maybe you want to bake delicious bread as your day job and write poetry on the side. Sounds simple enough: and yet it is anything but simple to become an artisan bread baker or to have energy left after a day of hard labor to tackle poetry. Even the clearest life plan is likely to founder on the shoals of reality.

The short answer to this dilemma is that life is not a romance. We can do an excellent job of identifying our meaning needs and making every effort to construct a life that matches that vision and still end up in an imperfect situation in which meaning hangs by a thread. Yet this is our success! It would be a greater success to have our efforts produce the exact results that we craved, but too much about life is out of our control for that to happen every time. Our steady diet of movies with happy endings blinds us to the existential fact that while we are here we must deal with the facts of existence and the bite of reality. The universe is not designed to provide you or me with meaning. Life is not a romance.

Maybe you have decided to make meaning by teaching youngsters. You nevertheless can't control your principal's temper, the

limitations of your mandated curriculum, or the financial difficulties of your school district. You can't change the fact that
your work pays a tenth of what any Wall Street analyst can earn.
You can't control the fact that your students come in sick all winter and that you get the flu more often than anyone you know. It
is a meaning drain that your summer vacation has been shrink-
ing, since you calculated in that vacation time when you made this
meaning investment. In a hundred ways large and small, your
investment in classroom teaching is threatened.

Ideally, we would get the proper meaning results from having made our strong and resonant meaning choices. In reality, we
get mixed results. Yet we have to call these limited successes real
and take pride in our efforts, because we did exactly what constitutes authentic living: we made value-based decisions and tried
to live up to them. It should therefore be abundantly clear why
you might feel simultaneously proud and blue. You are making
meaning, but you may get a much smaller payoff than you
expected. As we reckon with meaning shortfalls of this sort, we
have ongoing work to do. We may need to make additional
meaning elsewhere in order to shore up our primary meaning
choice. We may need to remind ourselves about the beauty of our
efforts and endeavor to detach from our results. We make our
meaning choices — and then the real work begins.

This is why your life ultimately may not make the kind of
sense that we are used to having good answers make. When we
do math, we expect an answer like "4." When we construct the
meaning of our life, we may come up with an answer like "I
intend to write my poetry, even though it will never pay; live in
love, even though I am only mediocre relationship material
(work on that); raise children in love, even though I am scared to

death that my critical nature will harm them (work on that); and continue with my day job, which I do not love much, by finding some ways to invest new meaning in it so that I feel like I'm not wasting my time — while simultaneously detaching from it, so that I am not burdened by its residue when I come home wanting to write poetry."

The above answer does not sound like "4." However, it does sound human, self-aware, and admirable. Would leading a life constructed this way produce anything like a lark or a straight line? It would not. How could it? Such a life would naturally look like the complicated, idiosyncratic lives that we see around us and would require countless meaning reinvestments, regular reinventing, and the kind of effort and attention that authenticity demands. You can feel smug when you do math. It is not possible to feel as smug about your life's meaning quotient.

Here, for example, is the actual meaning map of someone I know — let's call her Beverly. Beverly meant to become a full-time painter but entered the world of nonprofits so she could earn a living. She has worked in the nonprofit world for more than thirty years, toiling in the field of good causes and rising in the managerial ranks. About ten years ago she became executive director of a nonprofit that deals with environmental issues, and her specialty is saving birds. She does not actually like birds all that much — not living, breathing birds, at any rate — and would much rather be involved in some other cause. But this is where she's landed.

Every day she thinks to herself, "I would really prefer to run a different nonprofit with a more congenial mission." But her next thought is, "Still, I don't want to uproot myself again or deflect myself from my first love, which is painting." So each day she works hard to save birds, generating the kind of enthusiasm that workplaces generate but feeling essentially blank and empty — very like many of the people with whom she daily comes into contact in the nonprofit world. Like her, they know that they are "on the side of good," but what they feel, as they go about their business of finding a family enough money to buy a first home or supporting a young scientist with his dissertation research, is an abiding sense of drudgery and boredom.

Why can't the human spirit soar simply because our goals are humane and laudable? Apparently, we are not built that way. At any rate, Beverly's day job is not her primary meaning container, and while it provides her with a nice living, it is actually a meaning drain. Where does she make her important meaning investments? In her paintings — of birds! Real birds do not move her, but she loves painting surreal images of imagined birds. This should remind you of the anecdote that opened this chapter, about the collector who purchased a painting of a barn and not the actual farm of which the barn was a part. Where we decide to make our meaning investments is personal and idiosyncratic and does not follow any logic except human logic. Beverly is not inclined to spend one minute in her lovely garden watching real robins or sparrows, not when she could be in her studio conjuring imagined birds.

To add an extra dollop of absurdity to her picture, Beverly also loves roast chicken and smoked duck. Hers is an odd kind of laughter as she tallies her personal meaning sheet: saving birds without enthusiasm and painting them and eating them with great gusto. A little ironic laughter is certainly appropriate: laughter at how the universe has built us, as creatures who must earn our sense of heroism and who can only find such convoluted ways of doing so. Does it make sense to love making surreal paintings of birds, to not care much about actual birds even though saving them is your day job, and to eat chicken for dinner? Yes, it makes perfect human sense. This is the logic of our species, not of syllogisms.

Beverly's situation may not be yours, but I am sure that you will recognize it as a quintessential human situation. This is how we endeavor to make meaning; these are the curves in the road that threaten us with smashups. And naturally this is just the tip of the meaning-making iceberg. Not only will your path look idiosyncratic, but you will encounter a vast array of special meaning issues that flow from the choices you make. Visual artists, for instance, often experience existential pain knowing that individuals will own their paintings — that some collector will squirrel this or that painting away, make a fortune from it as it appreciates, refuse to share it for a museum show, and so on. How strange to imbue an object with meaning and then have it vanish into a psychiatrist's den or the guest bedroom of a magnate's yacht. This, however, is a visual artist's precise existential reality.

We could spend chapters investigating the special meaning issues of lawyers, flight attendants, househusbands, or television anchors. What about re-creative artists like actors and musicians who must deal with the feeling that they are "only" serving the meaning needs of others — the composer, the screenwriter, the director — and who often decide that they must create as well as re-create: that they must write and mount their one-woman show or put out an album of their own music? What about the particular meaning issues that confront the youth educated abroad who returns to his village, the fisherman confronted by an ever-dwindling supply of fish, or the police officer of forty years who must now retire?

You can see why you must nominate yourself as the hero of your own story. It is your right and obligation to make idiosyncratic meaning choices, but asserting that right and meeting that obligation only launch you onto an arduous path of lifelong effort. Time and again you will find yourself dissatisfied with your meaning results, shaken by new meaning problems, confounded by the dynamic complexity of your competing meaning interests, and exhausted by the work required to live authentically. Only a hero would bother with this. An ordinary person would settle for gods and greeting card maxims.

CHAPTER TEN

We Maintain
Meaning

(Daily and Over the Long Haul)

Making meaning is a genuine art form that requires daily attention and lifelong apprenticeship. There will never be a time when you become a complete master of meaning or when meaning becomes permanently settled. Just when you think you have learned all the intricacies of meaning, a new meaning development arises or a new meaning crisis occurs that makes you wonder if you've mastered anything at all. Your mate becomes very sick, or you suddenly lose all interest in your life's work, or a cloud passes across the sun, and for no reason that you can name, the meaning of your life changes. These staggering blows can and will occur. You can't gain the sort of mastery that guarantees your ability to deal with every meaning event with equanimity — but you can come as close as a human being can come.

You do this in all the ways we've been discussing. One of

these many ways is by coming to your own thoughtful understanding of the distinction between *making* meaning and *maintaining* meaning. What distinguishes one from the other? You decide to make meaning by writing a novel; you maintain that meaning effort by actually writing it. You maintain meaning on those days when you fear that your novel is awful, when the writing won't come, when you have to attend to other duties and responsibilities, when your in-laws visit for a week, when you doubt your writing abilities or your chances in the marketplace: that is, at all those times when you aren't in the trance of working and aren't actually writing your novel. Here is how Adam, a writer, articulated the difference:

> When I'm looking to start another writing project, I am many things: excited, passionate, and also anxious and sometimes frantic to get a fix on the idea and to get going on it. I long to be doing whatever it is, and I can't wait to start the adventure. Actually deciding on the work and beginning it relieves some of the pent-up energy, and I feel great moving into the "doing" phase. I feel myself always searching and discarding potential new ideas for projects, even when I have several projects under way in various stages. It's as if I'm always trying to make meaning ahead of time by keeping a mental project to-do list as well as folders for developing ideas. Making meaning feels as if it requires more physical effort on my part: it is mental activity, physical action, and so on.
>
> Maintaining meaning is more of a long-term emotional effort; there must be a well of discipline and confidence available in order to see the project to completion. Maintaining meaning also requires that I nurture myself with positive self-talk when I can't make it to the page for days or weeks at a time. When I'm maintaining, I'm reminding myself that it's

okay to keep trying, okay to move forward slowly, okay to keep returning when I can. It's very important for me not to beat myself up during this stage, or I hit a meaning crisis, where the lack of doing or the inability to move forward flips me into doubt about the project.

Let's say that you maintain a creativity practice and get to your painting first thing every day. You paint for two hours and then go off to your day job. Because you have painted for those two hours, not only have you made meaning, but you have built up sufficient meaning capital that the rest of the day can feel half-meaningless and you won't feel overly disturbed. If you do feel disturbed mid-afternoon by your nineteenth meaningless task in a row, you remind yourself that in a mere fourteen hours you get to actively make meaning again in your studio. During your studio time, you make meaning; at your day job, you actively maintain meaning by getting a grip on your mind and reminding yourself that another meaning opportunity is just around the corner.

Laura explained her take on this:

Meaning-making is the activity I engage in so that my life has meaning and purpose. Maintaining meaning refers to the rest of the time when I'm not actively doing something "meaningful." It's the many ways that I manage to maintain a sense of meaningfulness, even though nothing meaningful per se is happening. Twenty-something years ago I became a social worker because I felt that I had to do some kind of meaningful work while trying to be a writer. Doing menial work to support myself just seemed like a waste of too much time. It turned out to be a good decision because it feels meaningful to help people, and it also feels meaningful to write. As long as I spend some time each day doing something meaningful, whether it's working with clients, writing, being with my family, or any of the others things that I value, I seem to be able to endure those parts of the day that just can't seem to be imbued with any meaning.

Audrey construed the distinction this way:

> I see meaning-making as the physical process of writing a grant proposal: the time that I am actually getting the words on the page. I see meaning maintenance as the preparation of a contextual reality that allows, nurtures, and encourages the active process. When I am making meaning, I am actively in the process of going deep and coming back with a way to support our foundation. I am not researching, not doing any pondering, not solving a major day-to-day foundation problem. Some work is deeper and more intense than other work; that's where it feels like the meaning gets made. Some work drains the energy reserves more than other work, and that's when I consciously have to maintain meaning. I think that part of my maturity and existential awareness is the ability to notice this split and to pay attention to both states, to the state when the meaning gets made (and to try to maximize that) and to all the other times when meaning must be maintained and everyday things must get done.

Ralph, a lawyer, added:

> Parts of my lawyer life feel meaningful to me, and others don't. I can make additional meaning by the attitude I adopt: if I stand in relationship to my clients one way, I feel more present, grounded, and authentic, and those encounters feel meaningful, but when I treat my clients as ciphers, then meeting with clients becomes a real chore and a meaning drain. So there are really three states, as I see it: those times that feel meaningful without any work on my part (when I'm in court,

which I love); those times that I can make more meaningful by
the attitude I adopt and the intentions I hold; and those times
(far too many of them) when I am doing routine work that I
can't hand off to someone else or when I'm dealing with
bureaucracies, which seem to exist to drain the meaning right
out of me. Those times I have to consciously maintain meaning, because I am quick to get depressed, and if I don't watch
it — even for a day — I can start to sink. So I tell myself, "This
too shall pass," and try to remember that my life is really quite
full of meaning — except for several stupid hours every day.

Leslie, a poet, put it this way:

> Poetry is a primary meaning-making effort of mine. Where
> my need to maintain meaning comes in is when I have to talk
> myself out of believing that I cannot solve all the problems that
> come with writing poetry. I maintain meaning by showing up
> to write every morning first thing. I maintain meaning by car-
> rying the poem I am working on with me at all times, so that
> I can steal minutes from my workday to engage with it and
> even work on it over lunch. I maintain meaning primarily by
> persistence. Persistence is the key: the tortoise always wins the
> race, in this case, the meaning race.

If too little in your day can be made to feel meaningful,
because your job refuses to serve your meaning needs, because too
many competing duties and demands eat up your time, because
you've boxed yourself into a corner where your time and your
life are not your own, or for any combination of reasons, you
must change your life and, by changing your life, increase your
meaning options. If you are in an untenable situation, you make
meaning by changing the situation. A master at detachment and
mindfulness might be able to turn any sow's ear of a situation into
a silk purse of meaning; that may even be the existential ideal.

However, for most of us reality matters, and it is our circumstances that must change.

If this is your situation, that you find yourself prevented from making meaning by the contours of the life you've constructed, then your obvious, primary meaning-making task is to construct a new life. Naturally, this isn't easy to do. But it's absolutely necessary. Making meaning means manifesting your values in concrete ways, including, first of all, in the life you construct. If you have boxed yourself into a corner that is now defined by its sense of meaninglessness, you can stand pat and consider life meaningless, or you can make meaning by constructing a new life.

If you are lucky, you will not have to completely reinvent yourself. Let us hope that you can make sufficient meaning right now, in the context and contours of your present life, by identifying your cherished values, coming to new meaning conclusions, and taking action on those conclusions. But if more is needed, then that is the more you must do. You can bite your lip and say, "Just twenty more years in this boring job, and then I'll retire and *finally* get to make some meaning." That is your choice. But be prepared for twenty years of existential depression.

Once you've constructed a life in which meaning is a possibility, you make as much meaning as you can, remembering that not every hour has to be devoted to active meaning-making for you to feel happy. Make some meaning; take a nap; watch a television show; make some more meaning. You make meaning by turning your value-based choices into actions; you maintain meaning by reminding yourself of your intentions even as the sky turns gray or you feel compelled to take a very long bath. It is up to you to learn how much meaning is enough; how to make that exact amount; and how to keep the whole enterprise afloat, even on days that blow in an ill wind. Isn't this a beautiful art?

YOUR VOCABULARY OF MEANING

Another vital step in the process of maintaining meaning is acquiring a useful vocabulary that allows you to communicate with yourself and others about the meaning realities of your life. Without this vocabulary of meaning, you can't identify what is actually going on. If something disturbing is happening and you can't identify it as a meaning crisis, how will you handle it? You may misidentify it as "depression" or a "work problem" or a "relationship issue" and head yourself in the wrong direction. If you possess the language to call it a meaning crisis, then you know what to do: you know to make new meaning and right your course.

Sarah, a teacher, described her experience:

All my life I've struggled with meaning. I would look at others doing the things our culture considers normative and wonder how those things could be meaningful to them. From there I would usually progress to wondering what was wrong with me that those things held no meaning for me. Over and over again I've struggled with bouts of depression arising from this misunderstanding. As I look back, I can see how these down times have been the result of meaning crises, not psychological problems — a label both I and others have used to identify what I was experiencing. Having a personal vocabulary of meaning is profoundly important. I feel like I can now guide myself through the undertaking of making meaning. With this vocabulary of meaning in place, I have a whole new understanding of life and my place in it.

How do you acquire this vocabulary of meaning? The process is dramatically simple, except that you may be hampered by self-consciousness. If no one else is saying, "You know, I invested all day yesterday with meaning by working on my novel from 6:00 AM until dinnertime," you may find it hard to say such a thing, either to yourself or out loud. But if you can overcome your feelings of awkwardness and self-consciousness, just as you overcome them to speak any new language, the rest is easy — because the vocabulary will make perfect sense to you.

Try on the following terms for size, flesh them out, and fill them with your own understanding: *making meaning, investing meaning, reinvesting meaning, divesting meaning, meaning adventure, meaning container, meaning crisis, meaning conflict, meaning disturbance, meaning drain, meaning effort, meaning enthusiasm, meaning event, meaning frustration, meaning intention, meaning leak, meaning loss, meaning opportunity, meaning potential, meaning spark, meaning substitute, meaning threat, meaning vacuum,* and *meaning wound.* Thoughtfully consider each term. Then begin adding your own words and phrases. In the course of an afternoon you could have a vocabulary of meaning in place, and all that would be left to do would be to use it.

How would you use it? First of all, in conversation with yourself: "Visiting my parents is a considerable meaning drain, because my father still harps on how little money I'm earning from my music, and my mother can't get over that I'm not married or interested in having children. Because it is such a meaning drain and almost always precipitates an existential depression that takes me a month to get over, I am going to skip Thanksgiving this year. And I am going to skip it without feeling guilty, because avoiding meaning drains is crucial to my emotional health. At the same time, I am going to make a new meaning investment in my CD and exhaust myself in its service over the long Thanksgiving weekend. If I can make some meaning there and also avoid the meaning drain of going home, I will have created something like a perfect weekend, existentially speaking!"

You also use it in speaking with others, even if they don't share your vocabulary. For instance: "Hi, Mark, I wanted to tell you about the meaning adventure I embarked on last April. I had it in mind to make a little meaning by writing a song and singing it at the May rally that I told you about. Just going would have been meaning enough; but I wanted to invest the march with a little additional meaning by writing this song that I've had in mind for months and then singing it to just the right audience. A meaning opportunity arose when that snowstorm hit and school was closed and I got two days off teaching and I invested those days with tons of meaning by getting up early every morning, dealing with my doubts about my songwriting skills and my singing talent, and sitting there at the keyboard and actually writing the darn song! It was a real meaning effort, and I ended up exhausting myself, so I had to sleep a lot the next day, but in the end I got the song written, got to sing it for ten thousand people, and it became one of the great meaning events of my life."

These terms are only a small part of what may one day become a large vocabulary of meaning that we employ to meet every situation we face and to converse with one another with robustness and clarity. We shall see. For now, there is individual work for you to do on your own vocabulary of meaning. Create a vocabulary that allows you to effectively communicate with yourself about meaning so that, for instance, when the work you do begins to feel meaningless, you have a language to employ to help you deal with that crisis; when your siblings act as meaning drains, you know how to frame for yourself what you are experiencing; when you feel the urge to spend a month in the Brazilian jungle, you can avoid the language of supernatural enthusiasms and dub it a meaning adventure and not a spiritual adventure.

This last example should alert you to an additional reason why adopting a vocabulary of meaning is so important. Without it, you are stuck with the vernacular of our culture, a culture that is keen to call ordinary activities and events "spiritual." A person who devotes her life to helping orphans is not a spiritual person; she is an ordinary person who has decided to make meaning in an ordinary way that happens to be a way that we value. We might want to applaud her efforts, give her an award, and thank her in any heartfelt way that we like — without adding supernatural language to our thanks. When you have a vocabulary of meaning in place, you are inoculated against using supernatural language and have a way of deconstructing cultural idioms of spirituality. Your cousin says, "I had a spiritual experience"; you reply, "Oh, you had a meaningful experience. How nice for you!" Your co-worker says, "I've never had a more spiritual time than when I visited the formal gardens of England!" You reply, "Really? What was meaningful about that experience?" In this way you keep yourself supernatural-free and help others move in the direction of rationality.

MEANING AS WELLSPRING
AND RENEWABLE RESOURCE

You can also help yourself maintain meaning by conceptualizing meaning as a deep, inexhaustible wellspring and as an infinitely renewable resource. It is exactly those things. Today it may not seem meaningful to you to sit by the pond and feed the ducks, since you have too much you want to do; sixty years from now — or tomorrow, for that matter — you may decide that sitting by the pond for an hour or two is abundantly meaningful. At nine in the morning the meaning that springs to mind might be to fight an injustice; at ten, to send your daughter at college a sweet note; at eleven, to work on the song you're writing; at noon, to stretch and write for another hour; at one, to pass on meaning and pay some bills; at two, to resume fighting that injustice; and so on.

To think of meaning as something to find — something like a lost wallet or a lost ring — is to picture meaning as a very paltry thing indeed. In this mental model, meaning is so small a commodity that you can acquire it by taking in a guru's lecture or by sitting cross-legged in a dark room. You weren't sure what was meaningful. You listen to a guru. Now you know. Really? And what if you didn't tape the lecture and happen to forget what he said? Is meaning lost to you again? And what if you did tape it: Do you have to listen to the tape constantly to extract meaning? Is that the way you intend to construe meaning?

Meaning is nowhere out there. What if you discovered that the meaning of life was to stand on one foot while singing show tunes? What if you discovered that the meaning of life was to praise a one-armed man who lived in a faraway land? Would you find such revelations particularly exciting? There is no way to complete the sentence "The meaning of life is . . ." without producing a small, sad result. If meaning were the sort of thing that you could tag on to the end of a sentence, it would not be worth considering. Fortunately, it is not that sort of thing at all.

Meaning is a wellspring. You make it; it comes out of you; it is new each day; it is infinitely variable. It comes in every color and every tune. It arises one day one way because today you are valuing this; it arises the next day in another way because you are valuing that. It is also a renewable resource: you make it out of nothing but your own decision to represent yourself well and play the hero in your own story. And while it comes from nothing, it becomes like iron. You wake up each morning because nature renews you that way, you arise, you pull out your next meaning decision, and you make your next meaning investment.

Marcia explained how her take on meaning shifted:

> As I began to see that meaning was a wellspring I felt more connected, hopeful, and empowered. I felt a sense of connecting not only to a particular meaning-making choice but also to a deeper awareness of the limitlessness of possible meanings and choices. I found myself at times visualizing journeying into a wellspring deep in the earth, traveling through time, traveling and shape-shifting into the awareness and viewpoints of other people, of animals, of trees, of energies that had taken a drink from the wellspring; they were like little vignettes of creation stories. I realized that I had been equating meaning-making with something heavy, demanding, responsible, but as soon as I internally agreed that meaning was a wellspring it not only shifted my understanding of meaning-making but brought on a lightness as well.

Dylan put it this way:

> Conceptualizing meaning as a wellspring changed my relationship to it. Like Old Faithful, I began arriving at my desk with a bubbling up of creative energy. I experienced a building sense of creativity during the days when, because of my other responsibilities, I couldn't get to my writing; then, on the days when I could, I found myself able to stay put for much longer periods of time. The image of an inexhaustible

wellspring helped me maintain meaning on the days when I couldn't get to the computer, and it helped me make meaning on the days when I could. It seemed to work on many levels, to deepen my connection to my creative work, to banish existential depression, and to help me do the ordinary, everyday things more lightly and effortlessly. I can't say why it worked that way — but the change is amazing.

You may suspect a clash of metaphors here: if meaning is bubbling up, perhaps it seems as if you are receiving meaning instructions rather than actively making meaning. There is no clash: meaning is indeed bubbling up, but *you* are the wellspring. You are causing the meaning to bubble up out of your intention to manifest your cherished values, to act as the hero of your own story, and to live authentically. This wellspring is within you, but it also *is* you. When you think about a problem for a long time and a solution finally arrives, it arrives to you but also from you. It was your neuronal activity, your set of experiences, your genetic endowment, and everything that you are that provided the answer. You got the answer — and you also provided the answer. Meaning is the same sort of thing. You ask for it, and it bubbles up.

CHAPTER ELEVEN

We Make Our Ethics

(As Active Moral Philosophers)

I've said it before, and I'll say it again: there are no gods. We arise from nature — and nature is not a moral entity. A person may feel compassion, love his children, grieve the death of a parent, lend a helping hand, and engage in behaviors that we might, on the basis of some of our ideas, call "right" or "ethical" or "moral" — but nature is not moral. Nature dictates that one creature eat another, it allows for and guarantees the extinction of species, and, most tellingly, it has produced us: human beings who can justify, rationalize, and believe anything. That nature is not moral is not some sort of special problem for the atheist, as believers like to boast — it is a problem for anyone who would like to live authentically.

A long time ago the philosopher David Hume articulated the argument that ethical conclusions can't be drawn from natural facts. That tigers kill gazelles isn't a "good thing" or a "bad thing": it is simply what is. That an earthquake devastates a city is not a moral indictment of that city, no matter what cruel zealots assert. Killing is neither good nor bad as an ironclad principle: killing to defend yourself is one thing, and killing because someone has hurt your feelings is another. To draw a conclusion like "killing is bad" is to commit what is now colloquially known as the "naturalistic fallacy," the fallacy that we can derive general principles about what ought to be from what is.

More recently, about a hundred years ago, a group of philosophers known as linguistic philosophers, championed by the British philosopher G. E. Moore, updated Hume's ideas by looking at the seductive nature of sentence structure. Because of the power of grammar, people can produce empty slogans (like "Don't kill" or "God is the answer") and stake out simple moral positions that sound splendid but collapse under scrutiny. Linguistic philosophers noted that the power of these utterances resides in their linguistic form, not in their truth. The phrase "God is good" says nothing about the existence of gods or the nature of goodness and everything about how our mind reacts to linguistic forms.

A sentence like "Spare the rod and spoil the child" is not a moral statement but a self-serving tool for exerting power and making meanness sound necessary. We can make things "seem right" and "sound necessary" because of the mind's penchant for nodding its owner's head when it hears authoritative phrases. It nods at "Thou Shalt Not Kill" because the phrase has a ring of authority. But of course the phrase is as empty as any slogan. Most of the time you refrain from killing, but when vicious thugs invade your home you reckon that killing is justified.

You don't need any formal philosophical training to appreciate the implications of these observations. The appropriate conclusion to draw is that you can't create ethical principles from natural facts, even if what you happened to know was what the universe was all about. Even if you knew *that*, you would *still* be obliged to decide how to act. You are obliged to act not on the basis of some slogan-size principle or some putatively god-given command but on the basis of how, having thought it through, you would like to represent yourself. You don't grab a handy principle off the shelf and truck it out to justify your inclination to act a particular way. Instead, you think like a moral philosopher, recognizing that there are no ethics to embrace but only ethics to make.

To be ethical is to *make* ethics, not to *mouth* ethics. Realizing this may prove unnerving at first, but it is ultimately liberating to accept that slogans do not get us to ethics. We must get there completely on our own, using the apparatus that nature has wantonly provided us, by putting everything up for grabs and making choices based on our best understanding of what we value. The exact movement required is to stop looking for guiding principles and a static ethical code and to step up to the plate as an activist in the realm of ethics, as someone who thoughtfully translates her personal understanding of the universe into a way of life that allows her to feel righteous and proud.

You decide what you want to value. The universe does not care about fairness; nevertheless, you may decide that you would like to advocate for fairness. You don't make "fairness" a static, mindless chant that you repeat in rote fashion: rather, you let that belief commingle with your other cherished beliefs, each with its own weight and resonance. You do exactly what any serious ethicist does, what someone like the framers of the Constitution did: you decide what you want to value — fairness, justice, equity, and freedom spring to my mind — and then you manifest those values by making ethics and by becoming a moral instrument.

My hunch is that you want the chance to be an independent, self-directing, and righteous meaning-maker and ethics-maker. This is your chance! You get to make existential magic, and you need no longer despair that there is no place for you in our mock-pious, bottom line–driven society. As an existential magician, a conjurer with amazing skills bestowed on you by the universe, you can create your own stepping-stones and your own journey, guided by your own moral calculations. You make your meaning, and you also make your ethics. Nature being what it is, you are the only one entitled to do either.

EVILDOER OR MORAL GENIUS?

Let's say that I see you and another person chatting in the middle of the street, and I also see a truck barreling toward you. I shout, but you do not hear me — perhaps the truck is drowning me out, perhaps you are deaf, or perhaps I am not really shouting and only think that I am shouting. I see that you are about to be hit, and I rush out and tackle the two of you and knock you to the sidewalk. We hear the screech of brakes, and the truck comes to a stop inches from where you were — meaning, presumably, that it would not have actually struck you, though it could be argued that my darting into the street alerted the driver and caused him to stop an instant sooner than he might otherwise have.

Both of you are injured by the tumble. Your friend thanks me and sends me a box of chocolates. You, on the other hand, sue me, saying that I had no right to tackle you and that I am responsible for your injuries. Not only do you sue me, but you sue me for a very large sum of money, on the grounds that you will never again be able to dance with the Bolshoi Ballet. We would have to agree that I had no legal right to tackle you and that in some sense I am responsible for your injuries. Most of us would also agree that suing me is not the right thing to do, even if my action ended your dance career. In fact, society has tried to grapple with this precise issue by passing laws to protect doctors who stop at the sites of car accidents from being sued by the people they endeavor to save.

Why provide this example? For two reasons. The first is that ethics looks exactly like this. Ethics is an interaction among human beings playing particular roles in particular settings. We can't imagine how a private could stop a war in which he doesn't believe, but we sense that a general could perhaps be more influential. So we set the moral bar differently for privates than we do for generals. We do not think that a spouse ought to be forced to tell the truth if that truth betrays her husband, so we enact laws to keep spouses out of that sort of jeopardy. We back freedom of speech as a tremendous humanist value while at the same time making hard and sometimes painful decisions about when that freedom can be abrogated. Ethics looks like this.

Built into our outlook and our laws is this central truth, that morality is not about repeating slogans or adhering to a simple set of commandments. Rather, it is about expressing humanist values such as justice and fairness in a context of competing rights and interests, conflicting points of view, and complex circumstances. Do you find it thrilling that the CEO of a corporation can garner hundreds of millions of dollars in salary and benefits? Or do you see it as an example of greed and legalized theft? Is a gallery full of drawings of nude women art, exploitation, or both? Should an available kidney go to the next person on a list or to a researcher on the verge of making a monumental medical breakthrough? Ethics looks like this.

The second reason I present this example is that our children should be given scores of these examples and be invited to think like moral philosophers. Even small children would be thrilled to wrestle with the ambiguities and complexities of real-life situations, where competing interests, competing values, and competing ideas play themselves out. What would we be doing in such discussions? Not trying to arrive at a determination of "right" or "wrong" in a given situation, but modeling for our students how to *think about* right and wrong and preparing them to become independent moral philosophers. We would be teaching metaethics: that is, what ethics really look like.

You will understand that our children are unlikely to be taught metaethics in a school setting. It is virtually inconceivable that children would be given the opportunity to think for themselves, since schools are conservative institutions designed to uphold the status quo. Principals, and the parents they represent, do not want to create a school teeming with independent moral philosophers. If a teacher promoted such discussions, she would be reprimanded and quieted under some pretext or other. Does this remark tug at your memory? You are probably thinking of Jane Elliott and her blue-eyed/brown-eyed classroom experiments.

In the wake of Martin Luther King Jr.'s assassination, Elliott divided her students into two groups on the basis of eye color. She told her blue-eyed students that they possessed superior intelligence and gave them extra classroom privileges. Soon the blue-eyed students began tyrannizing their "inferior" brown-eyed classmates. The next day Elliott reversed their roles, and the brown-eyed students became the oppressors. One result of this brave experiment was that Elliott and her students were harassed and called names by the town's residents; a second was that Elliott was forced to move away.

Society is not inclined to allow rich work of this sort to proceed. Objectors to such experiments in ethics, believers especially, insist that people must not be permitted to make their own ethics because they would opt for evil. This objection is absurd on the face of it, because human beings have *never* been invited to step up to the plate as moral philosophers. It is impossible to predict what would happen if we suddenly encouraged billions of people to decide what constituted righteous action. We have never invited people to do this, and we have never seen people making this sort of effort, so it can only be a matter of prejudice to predict disaster.

We simply do not know what would happen if a society promoted the idea of making meaning and making ethics. We have never seen such a thing, so we simply do not know what to expect. My hunch is that you believe, as I do, that if you provided children with the chance to think richly and deeply about ethics, helped them articulate their cherished values, and provided them with the opportunity to explore the genuine complexity of ethical action, you would be much more likely to produce a generation of high-minded ethicists than evildoers. Not only that, but you would produce a generation of realists who harbored no romantic illusions about the ease of ethical decision-making or the purity of anyone's motives. Unless you were afraid of being found out by your children, what more could you want from your educational system?

MAKING ETHICS

You make ethics by striving to manifest your cherished values in every situation. What are those cherished values? Just the obvious ones: love, goodness, fairness, integrity, justice, compassion, courage, decency, tolerance, and so on. These timeless humanist values have coalesced into ideas like natural rights, human rights, civil rights, and legal rights. We understand by these terms our attempt to articulate how humanity *ought* to behave — the word *ought* in that clause coming from our peculiar genetic inheritance that invites such concepts to flower.

"Ought-less" nature made a creature with so many neural connections that it is able to conceive of right and wrong. That is our situation, like it or not. Nature is not the sort of thing that can laugh or roll its eyes at this odd creature it has created, one primed to operate out of self-interest but built with moral sensors. We, however, can howl at our absurd situation. You have no reason not to opt for unbridled self-interest, except that you know that you'll despise yourself for not meeting your own moral standards. So you stand up for your cherished values, even if it is absurd to be moral, since standing up is the only way that you can earn your sense of heroism and avoid finding yourself repugnant.

You stand up for these humanist values with great dignity, gravity, and seriousness, even though it is absurd to do so. When you are confronted by religious values, you assert your humanist values loudly and in no uncertain terms. You do not enter into idle debate: a believer's arguments are unassailable and foolproof, since he is betraying his common humanity by asserting that his values come from gods. If, for example, he says that beating his child is god's way, there is nothing for you to say — but there is plenty for you do. In your role as prosecutor, you prosecute him. In your role as school counselor, you report him to child protective services. In your role as a human being, you decide how much of your meaning capital you want to invest in addressing this particular moral outrage.

What, then, is the difference between "making ethics" and the more normal-sounding phrase "acting ethically"? It depends. If by acting ethically you mean that a person gives full consideration to the ethical implications of a situation, modulating his desires, moderating his self-interest, and meditating on and then manifesting his values, there is no difference. But if by acting ethically you mean that a person pulls out a slogan-size principle and applies it smugly and mechanically, avoiding an encounter with the self and acting primarily for the sake of appearances, then there is a world of difference. The first is the way of someone who has nominated herself as a hero and has donned the mantle of meaning-maker. The second is the way of someone who only knows that he ought to look moral.

I think that the term *making ethics* is useful, despite its awkwardness. It captures the sense of engagement, encounter, and activity that is the hallmark of authentic action. Just as there is no meaning until you make it, there is no ethical action until you take it. You may have fine ideas about what might be the right thing to do in this or that situation: those ideas do not make you an ethical person. Acting is the only proof of righteousness. You stand up; you speak out; you take your licks; you blow your whistle. Each atheist leads by example.

To presume that a poor person, a beleaguered person, a marginalized person, a minority person, or anyone without means or time on her hands can't make ethics is an insult to that person. To assume this is to act as if making ethics is a leisure-time activity for people of privilege, something like throwing a party for the Black Panthers at some swanky Manhattan apartment. Nothing could be further from the truth. Anyone can make ethics — or refuse to. You can make them sitting on your tenement stoop, bent over toiling away in a field, or hidden away in the farthest village. This is not an academic subject for armchair philosophers. This is the only way that righteousness exists — by virtue of the fact that people are living their cherished values.

The atheist's way is a way of life based on embracing these cherished values and agreeing that meaning and ethics must be made. A person traveling this path endeavors to make meaning that is consistent with her ideals, according to her best understanding of what her life ought to mean. She can lay bricks, bake bread, or write symphonies, but she can't perform just any work or accept just any life. The life she adopts, whether it is laying bricks, baking bread, or writing symphonies, must reflect her sense that her cherished values are being translated into righteous action. Meaning and morals are inextricably bound together: we measure the meaning that we are making against our value system and judge whether or not our meaning efforts strike us as worthy.

All this is damnably hard to do, especially since so little in the world supports our efforts. Self-interest trumps ethics in almost every profession and organization. We do not expect a corporation to institute a recall unless they are caught red-handed. We do not expect a gallery owner to mind anything but the bottom line. We do not expect a psychiatrist to admit to not knowing what ails his patients. We do not expect a dry cleaner to confess to ruining our pants. We recognize exactly to what extent self-interest is the prime motivator and how everyone colludes in not admitting this obvious truth. As the people around us cynically go about their self-serving business, we are inclined to grow cynical too. In such ways are meaning crises precipitated: Why opt to affirm value while swimming in a sea of self-interest?

These difficulties are like a thousand-headed hydra battling our efforts to make ethics. We lop off one head, and another cackling head appears. Because this is our genuine experience, we must return to the core idea that only heroism will suffice. The atheist's way of making meaning and making ethics requires your bravery. It is not just that we must do the best we can; we must do it against these preposterous odds: that nature is not on our side, that the majority of our fellow humans are not on our side, and that parts of our own nature — the parts that would like ease, a stiff drink, a roll in the hay, a second home by the shore — are not on our side. All that we have on our side is that inner voice that knows better.

And that is enough. You hear that voice and you listen. You demand of yourself that you not shut your eyes to reality, that you not opt for a pretty path devoid of righteousness. Your commitment is made doubly hard because that pretty path is offered to you in a flood of daily advertisements, those artful combinations of materialism, hedonism, pop culture, and religion that produce the following gorgeous picture: sex in a big house to the sounds of a lilting tune, with a big steak sizzling in the background and the promise of heaven when you are done. You can have all this! The only thing you would lose is your self-respect.

So we opt for reason and for ethics, just to make ourselves proud. We do not shut our eyes to the facts of existence or to the realities of human nature. We say, "I take these values, and with them I make my ethics." The painter creates a world; the writer creates a world; and you create a world, your own force field of ethical action. This is at least as beautiful a creation as any symphony or poem — more beautiful, really, because without it, civilization would soon collapse.

CHAPTER TWELVE

We Stand
Firm

(Even While Consternated)

I hope that our discussion of meaning-making and ethics-making has made it clear why we must stand firm in disputing god-talk: god-talk is at once a betrayal of our common humanity and a barrier to both meaning and ethics. That is not to say that you rise up in arms when you are visiting your parents' home for dinner and grace is said or that you leap into the fray every time you hear some piety uttered. No one has the time or the energy for such vigilance, and no one wants to become a pariah. But you do need to pick some fights and then fight them. If you are upholding values such as justice, reason, fairness, equity, and decency — if these inform the meaning and the ethics that you make — then you are obliged to stand up to god-talk at least occasionally.

As hard as that may prove, fending off your own supernatural enthusiasms may prove even harder. We are all susceptible to committing our own idiosyncratic version of the supernatural error. Like everyone else, we have experiences that seem not only inexplicable but also as if they contravene our basic understanding of nature. It isn't that, because of such an experience, we rush to create a new god or jump on some god bandwagon. What we do is become consternated, aware that these feelings amount to meaning crises of a very special sort. You have an unusual experience, you stand baffled, and you must do something to restore your basic meaning orientation, or you risk succumbing to a supernatural enthusiasm.

I mentioned at the outset that I was intentionally conflating a number of traditions, among them the secular humanist, skeptical, freethinking, rationalist, materialist, scientific, existential, and atheist traditions. But in real life an atheist may hold as a core conviction that there are no gods while at the same time embracing ideas that to another atheist look unscientific and "as bad" as god beliefs. In exactly the same sense that there have been religious existentialists, individuals who embraced existential ideas about personal responsibility but then leapt in the next breath to gods, there can be — and there are — spiritual atheists or new age atheists, individuals who take a pass on gods but who imbue the word *spiritual* with special meaning.

Why would this happen? Let's take an everyday example. You are going about your business, making meaning, making ethics, and living as authentically as you can, and suddenly, out of the blue, you are grabbed by the thought that the universe is completely different from the way you had supposed it to be. A second ago you had conceptualized it as meaninglessly running its course; but now, for no reason that you can name, you no longer feel confident about your former belief. Out of nowhere and for no reason, you sense something "oceanic" or "psychic" or "mystical" or "transcendent" and stand dumbstruck and confounded.

These are the kinds of experiences that cause many atheists to want to keep the word *spiritual* in their vocabulary. I think that this is a grave mistake, second only to allowing god-talk to stand unchallenged. It is better to stand consternated and not understand an experience than to commit our version of the supernatural error. It is far wiser not to sprint from a momentary feeling to a complete revision of our basic understanding of the universe. If we do not stand firm here — with ourselves — we are in serious danger of backsliding into inauthenticity.

When we backslide this way, we begin to identify certain pursuits and moments as spiritual and others as drab and ordinary. We dub our meditation practice as spiritual. We imagine that climbing in the Andes would prove a spiritual adventure. We spiritualize — that is, romanticize — activities like writing in our journal. But a meditation practice is not a spiritual thing; it is just an ordinary human activity. Journaling is not a spiritual thing; it is just an ordinary human activity. Climbing in the Andes is not a spiritual pursuit; it is just an ordinary human activity. The second we internally (and unwittingly) announce that traveling in the Andes is spiritual and having a cheese sandwich with our daughter is not, we have devalued our time with our daughter and inflated the value of an Andean adventure.

Does eliminating all spiritual enthusiasms from your repertoire render life drab? Not at all! Life is a project to live, not a mystery to unravel. You can invest your trip to the Andes with any meaning you like, taking it as the chance to meet new people, photograph new images, eat new food, look up at new stars, carve out a needed break from your everyday routine, take in some beauty, upgrade your political consciousness, fill up on sights that will enrich your blog postings, create some inner excitement, and more. These are normal human motives, normal human desires, and they are plenty.

For the sake of authentic living, it is best to excise all spiritual language. I would be thrilled if atheists stood firmer and made a greater effort to avoid all supernatural enthusiasms. By falling prey to just one enthusiasm — say, a fondness for homeopathy, the racket whereby distilled water is pawned off as curative — you can threaten your health, weaken your mind, and set yourself off in a terribly wrong direction. If you get in the habit of allowing reason to prevail and human-size experiences to suffice, you create a life far richer than one held together by supernatural glue.

Whenever you have an experience of a certain sort, you get to name it. If an experience puts you in mind of your own humanness, your connection to a vast network of natural phenomena, and to mysteries that can't be solved, you can call that an existential experience, or you can call it a spiritual experience. Both these words are available to you. The first returns you to your path of personal responsibility, meaning-making, ethics-making, and authenticity. The second leads you down the primrose path to supernatural enthusiasm.

This is the difference between staring at the Ganges River, feeling something powerful arise in you, and returning to your fight against dysentery, on the one hand, or carving a totem to Ganga, the Hindu goddess of the river, on the other. If you call your powerful experience existential, you are likely to return to your meaningful work as a research biologist. If you call it spiritual, you are likely to fall to your knees and perpetuate mythology. The experience is exactly the same in each case: rich, powerful, human, and motivating. But how you interpret it and what it motivates you to do are completely up to you.

It is always easier to call such experiences spiritual, because that softens them and moves them in the direction of heavenly featherbeds and mysteries that unravel into happy endings. You have that choice; since there are no gods, no one can stop you from choosing the soft spiritual way. You could let a flower's beauty warm you, as if that beauty ratified a hidden world of purpose and goodness; or you could let a flower's beauty both warm you and steel you to the fact that you are the moral beauty in your life. You can travel by metaphor in any direction you choose. Be firm and go existential.

A UNIVERSE OF CONSTERNATIONS

Who and what isn't consternating? Some regular sources of consternation are family members who are believers and remain firmly in the fold. Because we do not want to make scenes, cause ruptures, or waste our time and energy, what we typically do is keep quiet as they enact their rituals, utter their god-talk, and share with us their supernatural enthusiasms. The dynamic is a cruel one: they have permission to do what they like, but we, to keep the peace, must remain silent. Since we are consternated by their views and their practices but have decided not to speak, we begin to dislike their company: on the one hand because of what we see, on the other because of how it makes us feel to hold our tongue.

Jack described his experience of this dynamic:

> The hardest part of being an atheist is not speaking up. I love
> my friends and family, but when my uncle tells my nephew

that he was a gift from God, when my mother is told that her late boyfriend is in a better place, or when a friend from university tells me she plans on sending her daughter to a confessional school, I really have to keep my temper in check. Not that I become angry at them, but I have the urge to speak my mind, and I know in the long run it would just ruin my relationship with those people. So I need to pick my battles. For instance, I don't tell my nephew that while his parents may regard him as God's gift, God is just an illusion. But I did write a letter to my niece for her confirmation explaining why I am an atheist and why I feel that's the right choice for me. Holding my tongue is the hardest part of it.

Lucy tells a similar story:

My husband and I have a large extended family, and many of them have drifted into a variety of new age practices that they think are so ecumenical, nondenominational, and innocent that they can be foisted on others and no one is going to mind. Sometimes it manifests as reading biblical passages "for their literary value" at a wedding or a birthday. Or my husband's brother will proselytize about some Hindu guru "living legend" whose latest book we just have to read or about some visiting Sufi dervish whose dancing we just have to see. He has no sense that these are religious figures — he just treats them as ecumenical brothers and sisters, all with "a common wisdom." To us they are all part of the problem.

My sister Sarah has to enact a ceremony before company meals that involves lighting a special candle, inviting family ancestors to partake of the meal (I rather think that our great-grandparents would be happy to avoid another string bean casserole), having us get in touch with our "'higher power" (Sarah is also in AA), and forcing us to listen to pantheistic poetry that personifies the wind and the trees. She has no idea how insulting this all is to a rational, antisupernatural person. She thinks it is just spiritual, beautiful, and innocent. How could lighting a nice candle and reciting a little wind poetry insult anyone? It can and it does, because it is just lukewarm, disguised religion and no less distasteful for being lukewarm and disguised. If I started our meals with "There are no gods and please pass the pot roast," maybe she would get it.

You may have just as many problems in your own home, when believing relatives visit. Linda told this story:

> If I go to someone's home for a holiday and they pray, I sit quietly and do not interfere or sigh loudly or make any other disturbance. But when we have a holiday at my house, they are not allowed to have a formal grace or any prayers because it's my house and they have to follow my traditions when here. Of course, this did erupt into a huge fight with my in-laws the last time they were here, not only over them wanting to pray at every meal, but also because they were trying to "witness" to my sister-in-law's boyfriend, and we do not allow proselytizing in our home. We haven't seen my in-laws since. I'm not sure what will happen this year when we visit them, because my husband says he is going to leave the room during prayers. It seems to me that family situations are often the most difficult moments for atheists. I know that we are the black sheep in our family.

Sometimes what we struggle with are the supernatural enthusiasms of those we love, a situation that is especially and profoundly consternating when a loved one's life is at stake. Mark shared this story:

> My girlfriend was diagnosed with Hodgkin's lymphoma, which is cancer of the lymphatic system. Her first reaction was to visit a naturopath, quickly followed by a visit to a psychic

energy healer. Fortunately, she never turned her back on Western medicine (which isn't to say that Western medicine doesn't have its problems!). She always believed that Western medicine would cure her, and she saw her other pursuits as "interests" or "why nots?"

I think this is another area where fear comes into play and a place where the masses can be controlled into doing anything, including paying billions every year for remedies that are no more than placebos. What would I have done if she had turned her back completely on Western medicine? Well, without resorting to a straitjacket, what can you really do? Especially in the case of cancer treatments, which themselves cause so much harm to the body? I don't know! Right now Cindy is taking her treatments and getting better; but every Wednesday she and her psychic invite Mother Mary and Baby Jesus to help cure her. If that were the only thing she was doing to cure her cancer, I know that I would be half-crazy with frustration and despair.

A variety of other social situations can also tax our patience. Marjorie recalled:

Last year I spent Thanksgiving dinner with a friend's family, and I was asked to say grace by someone who simply would not take no for an answer. It apparently never occurred to him that someone might not be comfortable with offering up a prayer. This, of course, meant that I had the choice between pretending to be religious enough for prayer and starting what would doubtless have been an even more awkward conversation for everybody, especially for the nice old woman who'd just cooked Thanksgiving dinner for me. I compromised by delivering a little speech without specifically mentioning a deity. That seemed to go down okay, except for the odd moment of silence before I realized that everybody was waiting for me to say "amen." What's really disheartening about this is that if I had been Jewish, say, there would be no problem about me saying so and politely refusing to eat anything nonkosher on the table. But saying that you're an atheist is like inviting controversy and disharmony, even when that's the last thing you want.

Then there are the consternations at our jobs. Vivian described her workplace:

My last job was with a roomful of Baptists who were some of the best people I've ever worked with, yet they made me so uncomfortable that I had to leave the position. I made many references in casual conversation to growing up as a strict Roman Catholic, so they thought that I still was one and pretty much left me alone. But having to listen to daily prayer meetings and discussions about how much they should tithe and gospel readings and getting tons of prayer requests through email drove me right up the wall. I still miss the folks there but I do *not* miss the religious stuff that I had to put up with every day.

What can prove most consternating for former believers is the nightmarish residue of belief. Laura confessed:

I have recurring dreams about having fights with ex-pastors and Christian family members who are trying to get me to go to church again. Usually these dreams are benign enough, but sometimes I have nightmares in which I'm being kidnapped by fundamentalists or I'm stuck in a small town in Tennessee (where I went to Bible school), and I have no money to leave. I hate that one the most. I've been an atheist since the early 1990s, and I still have to deal with what goes on in the dark corners of my brain.

Sometimes we struggle with occasional backsliding. Rachel described her experience with this:

> After being raised an Orthodox Jew, every so often I have to deal with Jewish guilt. I was on a rather bouncy flight from Boston to Detroit a few days ago and found myself wanting to pray. I thought, "Why bother, you know there's no one listening," and just like that the guilt crept in: "But what if there is someone listening? I could really be messing myself up here," and so on and so forth. Suddenly there was an agnostic rather than an atheist on that flight — or at least until we were safely back on the ground and I could be calm and rational once again.

Probably our greatest consternation is caused by what we see occurring all around us. Mark put it well:

> Currently the hardest part of being an atheist is dealing with the frustration I feel every time I listen to the news. Religion is dominating the conversation when it comes to politics, education, terrorism, war, scientific research, civil liberties, and privacy. All politicians are pandering to those of their faith instead of declaring that the separation of church and state was meant to protect us all. We're in a constant battle to protect ourselves against the dumbing down of public education with the religious push against science. Anti-Western, antifreedom, and antifemale religious sects are gaining strength throughout the world. Promising lines of research are being stopped because of religious viewpoints on life and the soul. Religious prejudices prevent whole groups from enjoying rights in partnerships and parenting. This is all very hard to take — and why should we have to take it?

This looks to be a moment when atheism is capturing the imagination of many millions of people. At exactly the same time, fundamental religious belief is growing unchecked. These two events are likely intimately related, as rational people are frightened back to their rationality by fundamentalism and believers dig in harder against liberty, justice, and reason. Possibly nothing is more consternating than realizing that this dynamic between reason and the betrayal of reason is not some dusty historical fact but our current and pressing reality. We must stand firm and ready ourselves for some pitched battles in the war for reason's survival.

CONCLUSION

We Find Life Amazing

(Exactly as It Is)

L et me summarize my version of the atheist's way. You adopt the attitude I've been describing: you announce that you are the sole arbiter of meaning in your life, you nominate yourself as the hero of your own story, and you give up all religions and supernatural enthusiasms. You expunge all language of that sort from your life. You stand up as a simple human being who must earn her own sense of pride and heroism, and you make an effort to identify how you want to represent yourself and which values you want to manifest.

You create a life purpose statement that, for the present moment at least, captures your best understanding of how you want to live. You decide how to implement your life purpose statement, fully understanding that there can be no guarantees about your choices panning out. You turn those decisions into actions, doing whatever is necessary to implement them, from walking away from your job to reestablishing contact with your sister to slogging through the writing of your first novel. You maintain a picture in your head of who you want to be, and you become that person.

You also do all the following. You become expert at noticing, embracing, and reducing anxiety, because you do not want to let anxiety get in the way of your meaning-making efforts. You become a cognitive expert and come as close as you can to getting a grip on your mind, extinguishing any self-talk that doesn't serve you. You become a relationship expert, a mood expert, an addictions expert, a mental health expert: in short, you strive to make yourself wise in everything human.

At every stage, you make decisions. You never say, "What is meaningful?" With the question framed that way, the answer is, "Nothing." What you are saying when you frame the question that way is that you are unwilling to choose the next ordinary human experience to back. There are only ordinary human experiences to select and nothing that is meaningful until you imbue it with meaning. There is only a choice to make, a best guess, an estimate, an existential decision. Are you unsure whether renting that studio across town and resuming your painting career will prove a meaningful avenue, given that you haven't painted in years? Who wouldn't be uncertain? You do it anyway, if it is your best guess that painting is a smart meaning choice. Want a guarantee? Join another species. Our species just makes decisions.

This is how you make meaning. There is no other way, no fancier way, no more sublime way. You decide that you will fight the current regime, and you fight it. You decide that you will love this man or this woman, and you enter into the relationship honorably, clear in your agreements, clear in the understanding that you both must pull your weight, certain that you will not be a pest, cruel, or anything less than you would wish to be. You decide something, and then you live up to it, letting your experience of it determine whether or not you will keep investing meaning in it.

Maintaining meaning is not some esoteric or magical process. We frame it in the context of ordinary human experience, we put aside our wishes for human nature, life, or the universe to be different, we spare ourselves the false high of supernatural enthusiasm and the painful low of distaste for reality, and we do the work required to keep meaning afloat. We invest new meaning here, we reinvest meaning there, we divest meaning from an enterprise that has let us down, all the while keeping our eyes on how we want to represent ourselves. We name and then accomplish our next heroic (but ordinary) task.

It is true that we will experience pain. It is also true that we can experience joy. It is true that we are obliged to witness too much injustice in the world. It is also true that we can stand up for our cherished values and make ourselves proud. It is true that what matters to us often involves us in great difficulty. It is also true that we can appreciate our human-size efforts. Our glass is completely full of everything, from the mundane to the exhilarating. We have a word for all this: *amazing*. We do not know why the universe opted to make a creature that can suffer from a toothache one day and rouse his fellow human beings to righteousness the next, but here we are.

If we possessed a range of experience bound by boredom on the one side and terror on the other, we might be inclined to throw in the towel and say to nature, "Sorry, this life you created isn't worth my time. I'd rather return my material (and, by the way, can I get a refund?)." But our endowment is tremendously rich. It includes the possibility of love and the reality of love. It includes the experience of beauty and the chance to create beauty. It includes a good nap one hour and an invigorating struggle to make meaning the next. It includes everything, really.

This is indeed amazing. That the universe has created a creature that can sit on her sofa, picture her future, and say, "I would like to spend a lifetime devoted to meditative sculpting" or "I would like to spend a lifetime exposing scoundrels" is worth a round of applause. It is a mundane fact that most people will not make use of their chance to make meaning. But, amazingly enough, that chance remains open to them for as long as they live. They can cash that chip in any time they want. That, too, is amazing. You may spend decades not engaged in the project of your life and, remarkably enough, that does not prevent you from starting now. You have enough brain plasticity left, enough courage, enough everything.

If we were to list every difficulty, crisis, and catastrophe that you will face in your life, we would paint one picture of your life, one that would seem unbearable. If we were to list every joy, pleasure, and delight you will experience in your life, we would paint another sort of picture, the snake oil salesman's picture, a picture of life as a bed of roses. Reality encompasses all of the above, and that is amazing in its own right. It is amazing that we can do philosophy, eat a ripe fig, feel sorrow, vanish into the world of a movie, dance, cry over a few drops of spilled milk, and rise to the occasion. Reality bites, but it is also remarkable.

Imagine a young boy or girl of sixteen or seventeen bombarded by what young boys and girls today are bombarded by: celebrity nonsense; forced piety on the weekends; endless sexual innuendo and sexual energy; the blandishments of gadgets and things; school subjects of no interest; nothing really demanded of them and nothing really presented to them that strikes a deep chord; their days filled with text messages, algebra homework, and gossip. They are self-conscious, body conscious, self-critical, and half-empty, since nothing around them is nourishing them. Are they in a good position to make meaning? Hardly!

Twenty years pass in the blink of an eye. They find themselves adrift, blue, confused, overwhelmed, indifferent, phenomenally busy, and radically empty: that is our contemporary adult. When were they supposed to find the way to stop and examine their situation? Who was there to speak up for their existential responsibilities and to explain to them the art of making meaning? They have learned certain realities — about raising children, earning a living, dealing with their dark moods, plunging back into the dating pool — but something central is missing. They are bereft of meaning.

A crucial step is letting go of god-talk, supernatural enthusiasms, wishful thinking, easy comfort, and the other blandishments of our fantasizing mind, a mind perfectly capable of turning a peal of thunder into god's anger and dappled sunlight into god's good graces. You step fully out of that language, banishing it from your mind, and step into the language of meaning. Instead of saying, "Where can I find something that will finally make me feel alive?" you say, "What great meaning adventure can I plan?"

This is amazing, and it is also daunting. For no reason that we will ever know, except in the limited sense that science will explain it to us one day, we have popped onto the planet aware of our means and our ends, aware of our tricks and our talents, aware of how little the universe needs us to accomplish and how much we can do, plopped down here exactly like clowns in an absurdist play, too foolish and too wise to be believed. Let us make our situation even more daunting — and even more amazing — by advocating for this precise paradigm shift and by encouraging an explosion of meaning-making everywhere, in our schools, in our professions, in our homes, and first of all, in our own lives.

LIVING THE PARADIGM SHIFT

We need many things in life, among them basics like food, water, and oxygen. Another of our pressing needs is to feel that life holds meaning. If we do not meet that need, we feel lifeless, listless, and even suicidal. How can we meet this crucial need? By reframing it as an opportunity to fashion a life that matches our belief system. Instead of seeking meaning, as if it were lost, or accepting received meaning, as if other people had the answer, we boldly make meaning and treat meaning as a decision. As soon as we decide that meaning can be made and that it is in our power to make it — right now, right here — we discover that we can meet this pressing human need for meaning entirely from our own resources.

We have missed noticing that a lot of what ails us is rooted in meaning problems and not mental health problems. Depression, anxiety, addictions, personality shortfalls such as a lack of confidence, persistent procrastination, and confusion about life choices all represent meaning-making difficulties. Transforming yourself into a passionate meaning-maker is the solution to these meaning problems. When you make that change, you alter your relationship to life and begin to heal the pain that meaninglessness brings. Making personal meaning is not only the key to authentic living but also the best path to psychological health. The instant you decide to make meaning, you start to grow healthier.

You make personal meaning when you uphold your cherished values. What are those values? Most people have never stopped to articulate them. The key to making meaning is learning how to identify your values so that you really — and maybe finally — know what you stand for and what you want to manifest in your life. Once you create a compelling life purpose statement that captures your intentions and begin to live that life purpose statement, then you feel confident that your important values are motivating your current behavior. You know exactly where you are, existentially speaking, and you feel calm and purposeful.

Your next five minutes can feel meaningful to you — or they can feel like a waste of time. This day can feel meaningful to you — or it can feel like another day of going through the motions. Your existential job is learning how to make meaning investments in the increments of time available to you. By learning the art of investing real time with real meaning, you learn a new life skill, perhaps the most important one you will ever learn. In this way you move from psychological motivation ("My mother didn't love me") to existential motivation ("This project matches my values"), freeing yourself from depression, doubt, and negativity.

The ability to make personal meaning often collides with the kinds of work available to a human being. You can become a doctor, a lawyer, a novelist, a baker, or a project manager, but you can't be everything and, whatever choice you make, you must deal with the realities that come with that brand of work. Great existential heartbreak arises when we throw ourselves into work that doesn't meet our meaning needs, that isn't as rich as we had hoped it would be, or that can't be sustained because it isn't rewarded or doesn't pay. When this happens, we experience a meaning crisis and must take charge of the moment, either by reinvesting meaning in our work (and meeting its precise challenges) or by making a new meaning investment elsewhere. What we must not do is stand defeated. Possessing a vision of what you want your life to mean, a sense of the activities that support your meaning needs, and knowledge of the art of making meaning, you create a working blueprint for your meaningful life.

This plan is infinitely flexible: you modify it as your values, your circumstances, and your understanding shift and change. Will you make the same meaning investments at seventy that you made at twenty? Maybe yes, maybe no. Might you value something more if it's suddenly threatened and might it recede in importance when its safety seems secured? Certainly. The essence of authentic living is that you treat life like a creative project every bit as beautiful as the symphony you might compose or the novel you might write. Your blueprint is your current working outline: your life is the actual creation.

You maintain meaning by holding the long view in the present moment. You may be baking a potato, answering an email, or waiting in line at the supermarket, but you still know what you stand for, what your meaning intentions are, and how you want to manifest your potential. Therefore you are calm, centered, and satisfied, even though what you are doing is routine or unexciting. By holding the long view in the present moment and by always standing ready to make the meaning you intend to make, you learn to switch gears effortlessly and turn directly, without theatrics or procrastination, to your most cherished meaning-making activities.

A savvy stock market investor needs to know when to buy, when to sell, which market indicators to believe, and what an idea like "diversification" means. In exactly the same way, a savvy meaning-maker needs to understand the language of meaning and be able to monitor meaning events in her own life: to notice when a meaning leak has occurred, to know how to make new meaning investments, and so on. *Investing meaning* is a core term in our new vocabulary of meaning, a language that allows us to talk to ourselves and to each other about meaning. If, one day, this new vocabulary becomes widely shared, we will finally be able to enter into fruitful existential conversation.

Each of us feels rich: we can think, we can create, we can form opinions, we can imagine, we can innovate, we can act — even heroically. If we are prevented from manifesting that potential — by our society, by our personality shortfalls, by anything at all — we get depressed and feel cheated. Passionately making meaning is the answer. By forthrightly announcing your meaning intentions, you begin to mobilize your resources in the service of your intentions. When you decide to matter, you provide yourself with exactly the right motivation and, as a result, you experience increased energy, creativity, and productivity.

To meet your meaning needs and align with your meaning intentions, you have to fearlessly expend energy, produce adrenaline, and grow productively obsessed when obsession is called for. Making personal meaning sometimes entails round-the-clock work on behalf of a cause, full exhaustion in the service of a creative project, or hard mental labor as you craft the strong thing you want to say. Even productive people harbor a primitive fear of expending their capital on work of their own choosing, saving exhaustion for their "day job." With a new willingness to spend your personal capital on your own meaning-making efforts comes a new level of motivation and commitment.

We accomplish all this under the banner of atheism, thankful that there are no gods to control us, undermine us, punish us, or divert us from the construction of a righteous life full of passion and purpose. When we hear god-talk, we reject it; when we see a supernatural error committed, we expose it; when believers betray their common humanity with us by acting as if they possess some special news about the universe, we exclaim, "How dare you!" We let the thousands of gods invented by humankind sink into the sunset, and we demand of our fellow human beings that they do not browbeat us with their fictions.

Ideas that were birthed during the Enlightenment led people to question the existence of gods, the rights of kings, and the nature of meaning. Now that we have had sufficient time to ponder the past several centuries, we are ready to describe a new individualism, one that matches our experience as actors in our own lives, responsible for creating our own meaning. We are ready to accept this responsibility, and we smile, in recognition of the astounding journey that we get to make as the creators of our own meaning. I hope that you will join me in supporting this paradigm shift by announcing — loudly, roundly, and first of all to yourself — "I make my own meaning!" No announcement is more amazing or more triumphant.

This, then, is my version of the atheist's way. I think that it is a realistic, unsentimental, arduous, and beautiful way that allows for love, good works, and human-size happiness. At the same time it avoids humbug, especially the crippling and dangerous humbug of god-talk. Take from my version whatever makes sense to you, and heroically fashion your own atheist's way.

Residing as you do in a universe without gods, you must take the lead in creating yourself, making your meaning, and living your ethics. Nothing less than your righteousness and your happiness are at stake. Aren't you glad that the universe has entrusted these tasks to you and not to some squabbling gods or mountain sprites? Good luck on your atheist's way — may you make yourself proud!

Notes

CHAPTER 1. WE HAVE OUR TRADITIONS

1. *The Gospel of Sri Ramakrishna* (New York: Ramakrishna-Vivekananda Center, 1985), 34.
2. *Kalama Sutta: The Buddha's Charter of Free Inquiry* (Kandy, Sri Lanka: Buddhist Publication Society, 1992).
3. William McNaughton, ed., *The Taoist Vision* (Ann Arbor: University of Michigan Press, 1971), 48, 51.
4. Joseph McCabe, *A Biographical Dictionary of Ancient, Medieval and Modern Freethinkers* (Girard, KS: Haldeman-Julius Publications, 1945).
5. Ibid.
6. Edward Fitzgerald, trans., *The Ruba'iyat of Omar Khayyám* (Boston: Adamant Media, 2005).

CHAPTER 2. WE LEAVE OUR CHURCHES

1. Richard Dawkins, *The Blind Watchmaker: Why the Evidence of Evolution Reveals a Universe Without Design* (1986; repr., New York: Norton, 1996).

CHAPTER 7. WE DEAL WITH MEANINGLESSNESS

1. Irvin Yalom, *Existential Psychotherapy* (New York: Basic Books, 1980), 419.
2. Yalom, *Existential Psychotherapy*, 421.

CHAPTER 8. WE CHOOSE OUR MEANINGS

1. Ronald de Leeuw, ed., *The Letters of Vincent van Gogh*, trans. Arnold J. Pomerans (New York: Penguin, 1998).
2. *Joseph Campbell and the Power of Myth*, DVD (Montauk, NY: Mystic Fire Studio, 1988).

CHAPTER 9. WE MAKE IDIOSYNCRATIC MEANING CHOICES

1. Eric Maisel, *Coaching the Artist Within* (Novato, CA: New World Library, 2005), 19–34; Maisel, *The Van Gogh Blues* (Novato, CA: New World Library, 2008), 37–65.

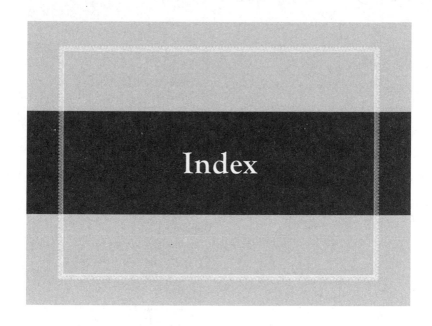

Index

A

Abu al-Ahmad, 14
addiction, 74, 91, 107
Adler, Alfred, 110
agnosticism, 35
alternative medicine, 159–60
anxiety
    avoidance of, 76–77
    choice as cause of, 75–76
    embracing of, 77, 166
    meaning/meaninglessness
        coexistence and, 91
    See also depression
Aristophones, 14
Aristotle, 14
arrogance, 70–71
Ascoli, Francesco d', 20
atheism
    defined, 5
    existential angst suffered in, 9
    family situations and, 157–60
    freethinking traditions and,
        15–25
    fundamentalism and, 162–63
    as movement, 10–11
    as reasoned way, 111–13
    spirituality in, 154–57
    tradition of, 13–14
    use of term, 10
    as worldview, 89–90
atheist's way
    advantages of, 4–5
    conversion stories to, 27–41
    current need for, 11
    doubting believers and, 25
    ethics-making and, 150
    fashioning one's own, 11, 175
    focus during, 43–45
    freedom as used in, 109–10,
        118–19

atheist's way (*continued*)
  god-talk vs., 3–4, 174–75
  meaning-making as central to,
    44–45, 95–96, 150
  "practical objection" to, 79–82
  summary of, 165–75
  taking comfort in, 1–2
  traditions integrated in, 2, 154
  as way of life, 2–3, 150
authority
  antiexistential nature of, 46–47
  meaning-making and, 51
  moral statements dependent on,
    142
  in religious tradition, 71–72

B

backsliding, 162
Bacon, Francis, 22
Bayle, Pierre, 22
belief, religious, 41
  atheist's way as alternative to,
    5–7, 25
  backsliding to, 162
  as comfort, 8–9
  contradictions produced by,
    84–85
  depression and, 79–84
  doubters in, 25
  existential angst suffered in, 9
  political impact of, 162–63
  residue of, 161
  as rote/reflexive way, 110–11
  as threat to human survival, 11
  See also religion; *specific religion*
Bible, 30–32
Biographical Dictionary of Ancient,
  Medieval and Modern Freethinkers,
  A (McCabe), 20
Blind Watchmaker, The (Dawkins), 36
blues, the. *See* depression
Bruno, Giordano, 22
Buber, Martin, 16

Buddha, 18
Buddhism
  conversion from, 33–35
  freethinking traditions in, 15, 18
  free will in, 107
  hierarchical tradition in, 71
  as "river" religion, 6

C

Calvin, John, 21
Campbell, Joseph, 112
Camus, Albert, 75
Catholicism, 5–6, 15, 161
Cecco (Francesco d'Ascoli), 20
Celsus, Aurelius, 20
Christianity
  depression and, 82–84
  god-talk in, 157–58, 159
  residue of belief in, 161
  See also Catholicism; Protes-
    tantism
"church home," lack of, 29
Cicero, 14
Coaching the Artist Within (Maisel),
  119
Confucianism, 15, 37
Confucius, 14
consternations
  backsliding, 162
  family god-talk, 157–59
  friends' god-talk, 160–61
  illness and supernatural enthusi-
    asms, 159–60
  political impact of religion,
    162–63
  residue of belief, 161
  workplace god-talk, 161
conversion stories
  Buddhist, 33–35
  Jewish, 39–41
  Protestant, 27–33, 35–37
  Taoist, 37–39
creationism, 30

D

David Copperfield (Dickens), 68
Dawkins, Richard, 36
decision-making, 115–21, 166–67
Delacroix, Eugène, 106
depression
 atheist's way as purported road
 to, 79–82
 dealing with, 84–87
 as "disease," 85–86
 existential angst as cause of, 9, 47
 meaning drains as cause of,
 134–35
 meaning-making and, 53–54,
 86–87, 170
 meaning/meaninglessness coex-
 istence and, 91, 95, 100–101
 religious belief and, 34, 79–84
desires
 "acting ethically" and, 149
 balancing, 4, 44–45
 identifying, 117
 meaning choices and, 110–12,
 118
 meaning investments and, 62
 meaning-making and, 44–45
determinism, 103–8
Dickens, Charles, 68
Diderot, Denis, 23
Dio Chrysostom, 20

E

Edison, Thomas Alva, 24
Einstein, Albert, 24
Elliott, Jane, 146–47
Emerson, Ralph Waldo, 23
energy healing, 159–60
Enlightenment, 174
Epicurus, 14
Erigena, John Scotus, 20
ethics, 52
 action in, 149

 bravery required in, 151
 complexity of, 144–47
 cultural distractions from, 151
 defined, 145
 education in, 146–47
 making, 143–44, 148–52, 156–57,
 175
 meaning choices and, 118
 nature not source of, 141–43
 self-interest and, 150–51
evolution, 35–36
exception, proving the, 109–13
existentialist thought/experience
 angst, 8–9
 atheism vs., 10
 awareness in, 130
 cultural marginalization of,
 45–48
 defined, 15, 52
 depressions, 80, 82–84, 93–94,
 132, 134, 139
 ethics-making and, 144
 freedom, 53–54, 89–90
 ideal situation in, 131
 meaning choices and, 166
 meaninglessness in, 93–94
 meaning-making and, 52–54,
 103–4, 120, 121–22, 125, 131–32
 motivation, 171
 religious, 15–19, 154
 responsibility in, 120, 169, 171
 self-nomination process and, 65
 spiritual experience vs., 156–57
 traditions, 2, 15–19, 154
Existential Psychotherapy (Yalom),
 93–94

F

faith, religious. *See* belief, religious
family
 antiexistential agenda of, 46–47
 atheist conversions and, 34–35,
 37–39

family (*continued*)
    authority and tradition in, 72
    god-talk in, 157–59
    illness and supernatural enthusi-
      asms in, 159–60
Fielding, Henry, 23
Fisher, Geoffrey, 16
Fitzgerald, Edward, 21
Frankl, Viktor, 94
Frederick II (German emperor), 20
freedom
    atheist's way and, 4–5, 109–10
    choosing thoughtfully as, 76
    existential, 53–54, 89–90
    meaning choices and, 118–19
    meaning-making and, 89–90,
      103–8
freethinking traditions, 2, 154
    atheism vs., 10
    Buddhist, 18
    Catholic, 15
    Hindu, 17
    Jewish, 16
    martyrs for, 19–21
    Muslim, 16–17
    Protestant, 16
    quotations from, 22–25
    Taoist, 18–19
free will, 103–8
Freud, Sigmund, 110–11
friends, god-talk by, 160–61
fundamentalism, religious, 162–63

G

Gibbon, Edward, 22
gods
    as explanatory device, 97
    nonexistence of, 1, 50, 62, 141,
      174
    subjectivity of meaning and, 50
    taking comfort in, 1
god-talk
    absurdity of, 3–4

atheist's way as avoidance of,
    174–75
    disputing, 153–57, 169, 174
    by family members, 157–59
    by friends, 160–61
    supernatural error and, 154
    as threat to human survival, 11
    at workplace, 161
grace, saying, 160–61
guilt, 83–84

H

Heraclitus, 14
Hinduism, 5–6, 17
Hobbes, Thomas, 22
holidays, god-talk during, 160–61
homeopathy, 156
honesty, 73, 85–86
humanism, 2, 10, 15, 145–46, 148–49
human race
    as product of nature, 1, 89
    meaninglessness and, 95
    rationalizing capacity of, 105–6,
      141
    survival of, 2, 10–11, 109
Hume, David, 23, 141–42

I

illness, supernatural enthusiasms and,
    159–60
insomnia, 100–101
instinct, 104, 110–12
Islam, 5–6, 16–17

J

Jonson, Ben, 22
joy, 167
Juan Chi, 18–19
Judaism, 5–6, 16, 39–41

K

Khayyám, Omar, 21
King, Martin Luther, Jr., 146–47

Koran, 16–17
Kuo P'u, 19

L

language
    of meaning, 55–56, 133–36, 173
    spiritual, avoiding, 154–57
    supernatural, avoiding, 136, 165,
        169
life purpose statement, 119–21,
    165–66, 171
Lincoln, Abraham, 23
linguistic philosophy, 142

M

martyrdom, 15, 19–21
materialism, 154
McCabe, Joseph, 20
meaning
    changes of, 77–78
    crises of, 90–96, 127, 133
    as decision, 170–71
    defining, 55–56
    idiosyncratic, 116, 121–26
    as renewable resource, 96,
        136–39
    seeking, 100, 137
    subjectivity of, 44, 48–52
    unaware, 117–18
    vocabulary of, 55–56, 133–36, 173
meaning choices
    decision-making process,
        115–21, 166–67
    free will/determinism debate
        and, 103–8
    idiosyncratic, 121–26
    life purpose statement for,
        119–21, 165–66, 171
    model for, 110–13
    proving the exception in,
        109–13
    self-definition and, 62–63
    value-based, 118–19

meaning drains, 134–35, 173
meaning earthquakes, 78
meaning intentions, 173–74
meaning investments, 65
    decision-making for, 167, 171–72
    defined, 63
    dreams vs. reality, 104–5
    life purpose statement for,
        120–21
    meaninglessness counteracted
        by, 94–95
    in meaning vocabulary, 173
    ordinary time vs., 56–62
meaninglessness
    counteracting, 94–96
    meaning maintenance and,
        129–32
    meaning-making coexistent
        with, 90–96
    meaning-making prevented by,
        132, 168–69
    of modern culture, 93, 100–101,
        169
    religion as comfort in face of,
        8–9
    supernatural error as poor at-
        tempt to deal with, 96–101
    of universe, 7–8, 72–73
meaning maintenance
    conceptualization for, 136–39
    meaning-making vs., 127–33
    in the present moment, 172
    process of, 167
    vocabulary required for, 133–36
meaning-maker
    decisions made by, 65–66
    as hero of own story, 66–69, 78,
        116, 165
    objections to donning mantle of,
        70–78
    self-nomination for, 65–69, 116,
        165
meaning-making
    announcement of, 174

meaning-making (*continued*)
 anxiety involved in, 75–77
 blueprint for, 172
 centrality of, in atheist's way,
  44–45, 95–96, 150, 175
 changes involved in, 77–78
 choice involved in, 75–76
 cultural apparatus for, 66
 cultural avoidance of, 45–48
 decision-making for, 166–67
 defined, 63
 depression and, 86–87, 170
 difficulties in, 170
 existential experience and,
  156–57
 freedom and, 89–90, 103–8
 meaninglessness as obstacle to,
  132
 meaninglessness coexistent with,
  90–96
 meaning maintenance vs., 127–33
 mixed results in, 121–24
 necessity of, 72–73
 as obscure term, 72–73
 paradigm shift in, 54, 101,
  170–74
 poor choices for, 51
 psychological benefits of, 170–71
 responsibility required in, 73–75
 self-awareness through, 119
 self-creation and, 9–10, 52–54,
  78
 subjectivity and, 48–52
medicine, Western vs. alternative,
 159–60
meditation, 155
Mill, John Stuart, 23
modern culture
 distractions prevalent in, 151
 existential awareness marginalized in, 45–48
 meaninglessness of, 93, 100–101,
  169
 meaning-making and, 168–69

 "spiritual" language of, 136
 supernatural enthusiasms sup-
  ported in, 36–37
Moore, G. E., 142
morality, 17, 145–46
 See also ethics
Moyers, Bill, 112
Muavia (Syrian caliph), 20
"Myth of Sisyphus, The" (Camus),
 75

N

narcissism, 47
naturalism, 10, 15
naturalistic fallacy, 142
natural rights, 148
nature
 as amoral, 141–43
 atheism and, 5
 human beings as product of, 1,
  89
 meaning-making and, 53
new age beliefs, 6–7, 154, 158–59
nihilism, 52, 54
numerology, 37–38

O

Omar Khayyám, 21
original sin, 83–84

P

pain, 167
pantheism, 158–59
paranormal, the, 6–7
parents, antiexistential agenda of,
 46–47
pattern-spotting, supernatural error
 and, 98–99
Petronius Arbiter, 14
Pliny the Elder, 14
premature closure, supernatural error
 and, 99

present moment, meaning maintenance during, 172
procrastination, 170
Protestantism
    atheism as alternative to, 5–6
    conversion from, 27–33, 35–37
    freethinking tradition in, 16
    residue of belief in, 161

Q

questions, answering, 116–17
Quran, 16–17

R

Ramakrishna, 17
Rand, Ayn, 24
rationalism, 2, 10, 15, 154
rationalization, 105–6, 141
reason
    ethics-making and, 151–52
    god-talk disputation and, 153
    meaning choices and, 110–13
    in religious tradition, 15, 20, 23
    self-interest and, 2
    supernatural enthusiasms and,
      156
    survival of, fundamentalist reli-
      gion and, 163
religion
    disadvantages of, 3–4
    ethics-making and, 148–49
    existential traditions in, 154
    freethinking traditions in, 15–25
    fundamentalist, growth of,
      162–63
    science vs., 162
    taking comfort in, 1, 8–9
    as threat to human survival, 11
    See also belief, religious; *specific*
      religion
responsibility, personal
    existential, 120, 156
    in meaning-making, 73–75

"river" religions, 6
Rubaiyat, The (Omar Khayyám), 21

S

schools
    antiexistential agenda of, 46
    moral education in, 146–47
science
    Bible vs., 31–32
    creationism vs., 30
    hypothesis-testing in, 120–21
    limitations of, 4
    meaninglessness and, 95
    religious belief and, 8–9, 31–32,
      97, 162
    supernatural error and, 98
    traditions in, 2, 15, 154
secularism, 2, 10, 15, 154
self-awareness, 119, 169–70
self-creation, 9–10, 52–54, 75, 78, 175
self-definition, 43, 62–63
self-interest, 43
    atheist's way and, 2, 4, 44
    balancing, 4
    enlightened, meaning invest-
      ments made in accordance
      with, 65
    ethics and, 149, 150–51
    human nature and, 62
    instinct for, 2
    internal discussion of, 44
    meaning choices and, 103–4, 118
    meaning-making and, 44, 50
    morality and, 148
    selfish vs. humanist, 10–11, 109
    subjectivity of meaning and, 50,
      51
selfishness, 52
self-nomination, as meaning-maker,
    65–69, 116, 165
Seneca, 14
Servetus, Michael, 21
Shelley, Percy Bysshe, 23

sin, 80, 83–84
skepticism, 2, 10, 154
spirituality
    avoiding language of, 154–57
    cultural focus on, 136
    as supernatural error, 155
Stanton, Elizabeth Cady, 24
Storr, Anthony, 24–25
subjectivity, 44, 48–52
supernatural beliefs/enthusiasms
    cultural support of, 36–37
    disadvantages of, 6–7
    fending off, 136, 153–57, 165, 169
    illness and, 159–60
supernatural error, 96–101
    atheist's way and exposing of,
        174
    atheist version of, 153–55
    dangers of, 100–101
    defined, 96–98
    reasons for committing, 98–99
superstition, 37–38

T

Tai-tsung (Chinese emperor), 20
Taoism, 6, 15, 18–19, 37–39
Thomas Aquinas, Saint, 15
tradition
    atheist, 13–14
    breaking with, 71–72
    freethinking, 15–25
"'Tzu Yeh' Song" (Kuo P'u), 19

U

Ulpianus, Domitius, 20

universe
    as amazing, 167–70
    as indifferent, 7–8, 62, 79–80
    meaninglessness of, 7–8, 72–73
    supernatural error as attempt to
        explain, 96–101

V

Valla, Lorenzo, 20–21
values
    ethics-making and, 143–44
    humanist, morality and, 145–46,
        148–49
    identifying, 171
    meaning investments and, 62
Van Gogh Blues, The (Maisel), 119
van Gogh, Vincent, 106
vocabulary, of meaning, 55–56,
    133–36, 173
Voltaire, 23

W

Way, The (Taoist concept), 38–39
Wilcox, E. W., 52
work/workplace
    god-talk at, 161
    meaning maintenance at, 129–32
    meaning-making and, 171–72

Y

Yalom, Irvin, 93–94

Z

Zen Buddhism, 71

About the Author

E ric Maisel, PhD, psychotherapist, philosopher, and cultural observer, is widely regarded as America's foremost creativity coach. He trains creativity coaches nationally and internationally and provides core trainings for the Creativity Coaching Association. Eric is a columnist for *Art Calendar* magazine and hosts two shows on the Personal Life Media network, one on creativity and one on atheism.

His books include *Coaching the Artist Within*, *Creative Recovery*, *Fearless Creating*, *The Van Gogh Blues*, and a score of others. He lives in the San Francisco Bay Area with his family.

Visit his websites:
www.ericmaisel.com and www.theatheistsway.com